W9-AOM-048

R 975.918 H341s
Harvey, Karen G., 1944-
St. Augustine and St. Johns County

WITHDRAWN

St. Augustine
and St. Johns County

Rockford Public Library

THIS ITEM DOES NOT CIRCULATE

St. Augustine
and St. Johns County

A Pictorial History by Karen Harvey

Design by
Barbara Buckley

Donning Company/Publishers
Virginia Beach, Virginia

A majestic triumvirate commands the skyline from the Ponce de Leon Hotel vantage. Beyond the well-manicured park in the center is the Alcazar, smaller sister-hotel of the Ponce de Leon. Completed late in 1888, the Alcazar was erected by Henry Flagler to accommodate less wealthy winter visitors. Architects Carrere and Hastings and contractors McGuire and McDonald were commissioned for construction of both Spanish Renaissance-style buildings. The Casa Monica, to the left of the Alcazar, was built by Franklin Smith between 1886 and 1888. Flagler added the Casa to his empire in 1889, changing the name to the Cordova. At one time a covered walkway above the street linked the Cordova to the Alcazar. A major portion of the Cordova has been converted into county offices including the board of education, board of county commissioners, and the County Court House. The Alcazr houses city offices and also the Lightner Museum. Otto C. Lightner purchased the building in 1947 to display his rare and extensive collection of articles from around the world. The collection was left in the care of St. Augustine citizens after Lightner's death in 1950. Photograph from the Library of Congress.

ROCKFORD PUBLIC LIBRARY

Copyright © 1980 by Karen Harvey

All rights reserved, including the right to reproduce this book in any form whatsoever without permission from the publisher, except for brief passages in connection with a review. For information write: The Donning Company/Publishers, Inc., 5041 Admiral Wright Road, Virginia Beach, Va. 23462

Library of Congress Cataloging in Publication Data:

Harvey, Karen G., 1944-
St. Augustine and St. Johns County.
Bibliography: p.
Includes index.
1. St. Johns Co., Fla.—History 2. St. Johns Co., Fla.—Description and travel. 3. St. Augustine—History 4. St. Augustine—Description I. Title
F317.518H37 975.9′18 79-19039
ISBN 0-89865-011-9 pbk.
ISBN 0-89865-025-9 lim. ed.

975.918 H341s
Harvey, Karen G., 1944-
St. Augustine and St. Johns
County

JUL 1 2 1988

For Kristina and Jason, whom I hope will develop an appreciation for the nation's oldest city, enhancing a love for their country.

Bay Street around 1880. Photograph courtesy of Margaret Gibbs Watt.

Nancy and Sally Pinkham stand before the City Gate in the 1880s with Castle Warden and a portion of the Abbott house visible in the background. The sign behind the women states: "$10 fine for driving or riding through the gates faster than a walk." Photograph courtesy of Slade D. Pinkham.

Foreword

Unknown to readers of the typical American history textbook, the first permanent European settlement in what is now the United States was not Jamestown, Virginia, in 1607 or Plymouth Plantation, Northern Cape Cod Bay, in 1620. That honor belongs to the subject of this splendid new book—St. Augustine, Florida. Founded by Spaniards under Don Pedro Menéndez de Avilés on September 8, 1565, St. Augustine proudly wears the mantle of first permanent settlement, oldest city, and cradle of Christianity in North America.

Indeed, by the time that the English Puritans splashed ashore at Plymouth Rock, St. Augustine was ongoing and vigorous enterprise with fort, church, seminary, six-bed hospital, fish market, and some 120 shops and houses. Though never powerful or affluent—she was several times sacked or destroyed by English forces, and for most of her Spanish occupation she depended for very survival on a subsidy, the *situado* sent annually from Mexico City—still she survived, no mean feat in itself. Spain called her "la siempre fiel ciudad"—the ever-faithful city. Except for a brief twenty-one year period under British rule, St. Augustine would salute the flag of Spain for two and a half centuries. Not until the year 2055 will the American flag have flow over St. Augustine as long as did the flag of Spain.

This, then is the city where western civilization first took root in our land; where missionaries first planted the Cross of Christianity and held hands of benediction over America's aboriginal inhabitants; where pioneer settlers and Franciscan friars erected our country's first schools, hospitals, and missions; where farmers cleared the first fields for planting, and ranchers tanned the first hides of cattle; where old Europe made its first beachhead for the tens of millions of immigrants who would follow in the centuries afterwards. Truly this is historic ground, and fully deserving of our notice as we pause to mediate on these pictures from the past.

Florida, and with it this ancient city, passed from the hands of Spain to those of the infant United States in 1821. Though still small, St. Augustine at the time was one of the most cosmopolitan communities on the southeastern seaboard. Not only Spaniards, but a sizable number of Minorcan families dominated in the town. The latter, a people of remarkable fidelity and courage, had come into the city during the British period (1763-84), refugees from an ill-fated indigo plantation at New Smyrna. Other residents, too, had remained in town from the earlier British period. There were Indians of several nations, and blacks, both slave and free. In the city that came under United States rule one could hear spoken in the streets a great many languages: Spanish, Catalan, English (often with a Scottish burr), Greek, Italian, Sicilian, German, French, Mandingo, Muskogee, Hitchiti, and Cherokee.

That diversity of population and language became less pronounced as St. Augustine moved forward into the nineteenth century and thousands of United States citizens came south into the city. Even with the ascendancy of the American newcomers, however, Minorcan citizens continued to hold important civil offices. A national constitutional crisis erupted over the issue of slavery at mid-century, and Florida seceded from the Union along with the other Southern states. Though more spared of war-time damage than was any other state of the Confederacy, in many places Florida experienced the humiliation of Union occupation. One of these places was St. Augustine. Certain of her sons' roles in the tragic conflict, called by some the Civil War and by others the War Between the States, is told in these pages.

It was in the post-war years that photography became a widely used recorder of people, buildings, and landscapes. The bulk of the photographs in this book date therefore from that period. As the Reconstruction years passed to the so-called Bourbon Era of the 1880s and 1890s, we can follow the camera as it captured the people of the city: the famous and the not so famous; the old families and the new residents; the first tourists, originally called "strangers"; the soldiers and Apache captives; and the community leaders—mayors, clergymen, businessmen, developers, and mothers of families.

When the city stood poised to cross into the twentieth century, the fifth that it would experience, its appearance was still much like that which greeted a visitor at the close of the Spanish occupation. Dominating the northern sea wall was the great Castillo de San Marcos (Castle of St. Mark), whose never-conquered bastions looked down on the inlet approaches. To the west and south of the fortress other notable structures from colonial times still stood: the City Gate, Cathedral, Government House, and numerous dwellings. By this date the old structures were partially eclipsed in both size and grandeur by the three extraordinary new hotels erected by Henry M. Flager: the Ponce de Leon, Alcazar and Cordova. Their presence against the skyline symbolized what would be the principal foundation of the city's economy in the twentieth century: tourism. From every part of the country visitors poured into the Ancient City, some searching for history and romance among the old monuments, others searching for sun and water along St. Augustine's magnificent wide beaches, still others searching for amusement at the new attractions that sprouted up on every side. Observing the city's concentration on tourism, some local citizens expressed their concern that St. Augustine was turning into what they called a "catchpenny town." Most of the citizens realized, however, that tourism was the city's economic salvation, if not destiny, and while they understood that it was the city's historical relics that attracted tourists in the first place, it remained true that the times were so good, and the visitors so plentiful, few felt any immediate need to worry that they might one day kill the goose that laid the golden egg. And so the tourist industry continued apace.

For a brief time, and concurrently with the rest of Florida, St. Augustine enjoyed a land boom. From 1920 to 1926 developers projected entire new communities in and around the city, on "rich Florida land," submerged and otherwise. Hit hard by the collapse of the boom, the city's tourist-built economy suffered again soon afterwards during the national depression of the 1930s. It revived somewhat, however, during the Second World War when Coast Guardsmen stationed in the Ponce de Leon Hotel and soldiers and sailors from nearby military bases flooded the city on weekends.

The years since 1945 have been a time of almost uninterrupted prosperity for the Ancient City. Again tourism was the reason. Save for brief periods when St. Augustine shared in the recessions that afflicted the country as a whole, her appeal to tourists remained strong, and numerous new businesses developed to service the visitor traffic. By 1959, however, not only the city's political and business leaders but also state government officials began to express concern that the original fabric of colonial St. Augustine was becoming so overgrown with new structures, many of which lacked architectural merit, not to mention historical conformity, that unless something was done to preserve, reconstruct, and restore the historical areas the figurative goose was indeed at peril. That concern coincided with the beginnings, nationally, of a strong preservation movement led by the National Trust for Historic Preservation and by Colonial Williamsburg.

This was not the first instance in this century, however, of concern expressed for the proper maintenance of St. Augustine as a state and national treasure. In 1936 a meeting took place in the city of what was called the "National Committee for the Preservation and Restoration of St. Augustine." The committee's membership included such important figures as Dr. John Merriam, President of the Carnegie Institution; Senator Harry F. Byrd, of Virginia; Dr. Verne Chatelain, of the National Park Service; and historian Dr. Herbert E. Bolton, of the University of California. Unfortunately, the committee's work, extremely valuable for its archaeological and documentary spadework, was brought to a halt by the outbreak of World War II. Then, in 1959 a new and fruitful initiative was taken jointly by the state of Florida, the city of St. Augustine, and St. Johns County. Under the leadership of St. Augustine native Senator Verle A. Pope and Governor LeRoy Collins, the legislature created the St. Augustine Historical Restoration and Preservation Commission, now called Historic St. Augustine Preservation Board. Chaired for the first ten years by local contractor and banker Herbert E. Wolfe, the Board inaugurated a rescue operation for many of the city's important historical buildings and sites, a good number of which are pictured in this volume.

Although the Preservation Board, acting together with the city and county, has a formal responsibility for preservation that is mandated by state law, it has never been alone in preservation activities. Long before the Board's formation individual citizens had acted to preserve and restore their historical properties. The National Park Service, custodians of the Castillo and City Gate, has its own long and distinguished record in this area. Perhaps no other agency deserves the measure of praise that is owed the St. Augustine Historical Society. The members of its board of directors, all local citizens, have served since 1883 as trustees of the city's bibliographic, cartograhic, documentary, and photographic record. Without the resources of the Historical Society the accomplishments of the Preservation Board would not have been possible. Without the same resources, it is not too much to say, this present book would not have been possible.

Within the pages of her volume Karen Harvey has produced a photographic story of the city, the best in my judgement that has been done. Here are the city's roots: her people, industries, buildings, sites, and many important events. Karen Harvey's is yet another means by which a community preserves its past. For many years to come both residents and visitors will learn through this book something of what it meant to live in this place many years, even centuries ago. It is to the compiler's particular credit that she made an exhaustive search, among families as well as in library collections, for the photographs reproduced here; many are published for the first time. Her book is a fine addition to the St. Augustine bookshelf. I am pleased to have this chance to recommend it.

Michael V. Gannon, Chairman,
Historic St. Augustine Preservation Board.

Five eighteenth-century houses are extant on St. George Street. They cluster here in their nineteenth-century appearance. "The Old House" on the left, displaying the familiar round clock, is the Paredes House. Sharing a common wall and chimney is the three-story structure known as the Rodriguez-Avero-Sanchez House. Beyond is the balcony of the Arrivas House, and across the street is the De Mesa-Sanchez balcony, which almost hides the Avero House next door. Photograph from the Historic St. Augustine Preservation Board.

Acknowledgments

This book is a tribute to a very special city. It is my hope that the historic ambience of this most ancient city will be conveyed through the visual imagery of these photographs.

Throughout the year spent compiling this pictorial, it was my good fortune to meet numerous native families whose roots sink deep in the venerable city soil. I extend my gratitude to those wonderful St. Augustinians who contributed precious photos and anecdotes passed down from former generations.

Another pleasurable benefit was working with and learning from professional and amateur historians who share the respect and love for this city which I have since acquired. It was through the useful suggestions and able assistance of Jacqueline K. Bearden of the St. Augustine Historical Society that this volume took form. She and several members of the Society were of immeasurable help during the months of research and decision making.

The cooperation of the members of the Historic St. Augustine Preservation Board enriched the material. My grateful thanks to Dr. Michael C. Scardaville, Robert W. Harper III, and David Nolan for architectural explanations and use of photographic material and research data as well as for giving so generously of their time.

Special mention goes to a delightful and informative woman at the Photographic Archives of Florida State University. Joan (Mrs. Allen) Morris assisted in the painful elimination process from the superb photographic material she has skillfully cataloged and filed.

For the quality of all my photos, I thank my friend and neighbor, photographer Robert Lange. His capable persistence produced more than four hundred excellent reproductions.

So many individuals contributed unique talents and special knowledge that all cannot be mentioned here. However, I wish to acknowledge the following: Eleanor Philips Barnes for contributing genealogical information from her wealth of documented evidence, and Sister Mary Albert, who I believe knows Father O'Reilly better than his contemporaries did. For a myriad of reasons I thank: Leonora Stoddard, Earl Masters, B. M. Hall, Mr. and Mrs. Clyde Hoey, Lorna Pacetti, Hiram Faver, X. L. Pellicer, Slade Pinkham, Janis Guerrera, Colonel Frank Persons, the *St. Augustine Record*, and all those whose names accompany their family photographs.

Three historians have given me special support: Dr. Michael V. Gannon, whose love of the ancient city lured him into an examination of these old photos, resulting in the accompanying Foreword; Dr. Thomas S. Graham, who offered valuable suggestions and whose research on the Anderson family and Flagler era was indispensable; and Albert C. Manucy, whom I consider my mentor and will say no more about except, "Thank you."

My personal gratitude goes to several people close to me. I thank my niece, Karen DeLette Haught, for typing, baby-sitting and assuming domestic responsibilities during the days preceding the manuscript deadline. I thank my friend Ann Hein for proofing pages and pages of script. Lastly, but most importantly, I thank my husband, John, whose patience, support, and infinite faith make all things possible.

Pedro Menendez de Aviles

Chapter One

The First Spanish Period: 1565-1763

Don Pedro Menéndez de Avilés, founding father of St. Augustine. A likeness of the Spanish conquistador and Adelantado of Florida was executed by Titian in 1574, the year Menendez died. This copy was presented in 1979 to Governor Robert Graham for the state of Florida by His Excellency Don José Llado, Spanish ambassador to the United States, and His Excellency Don Jaime Pinies, Spanish ambassador to the United Nations. Photograph of portrait from the State of Florida.

There is an aura surrounding the date 1565. It is a whisper implying importance, not the shout of the spirit of 1776. Every schoolchild recognizes the latter date as the era marking the birth of the United States of America; however, it is the former that signifies the founding of the first city of our nation.

The earliest recorded sighting of Florida is credited to Juan Ponce de León, who sailed along the sandy coast in the spring of 1513. He went ashore somewhere between St. Augustine and the St. Johns River on an April day, giving the land the name *Pascua florida* ("Feast of Flowers at Easter time"). His ill-fated attempts at colonization resulted in his own death in 1521.

It was not until 1565 that a permanent settlement was established. In that year King Philip II of Spain designated Pedro Menéndez de Avilés as *Adelantado* (governor) to explore and colonize Florida. The king specified that any settlers not subject to the crown should be driven from the land, a demand prompted by the news that the French already had a foothold in Florida called Fort Caroline. King Philip's selection of Menéndez was well calculated, for he was a superb sailor and a brave leader of proven loyalty who had previously served as captain general of the convoys to and from the Americas.

Menéndez's armada of nineteen ships and more than one thousand people sailed from Cadiz in June. On August 28, a day honoring Saint Augustine, Bishop of Hippo, Menéndez gazed upon the white shores of Florida. Only five ships remained in the fleet; others surviving the journey would join them later. As he sailed northward, Menéndez passed an outlet leading into a quiet bay. On its shore was the Indian village of Seloy, but Menéndez pushed on until he sighted four large galleons anchored at the mouth of the St. Johns River. This was the fleet of the French leader Jean Ribault, whose strong reinforcements for the colony had already debarked. Menéndez challenged the French vessels, only to see them scatter before him. He returned south to Seloy, and there he founded St. Augustine. By September 8, 1565, all members of the expedition had come ashore, and the momentous occasion was observed with much pomp and ceremony. Mass was celebrated, and the land was claimed in the name of the king.

Before the *Adelantado* could begin the development of Florida, it was necessary to eliminate the French threat. Menéndez accomplished the task swiftly by striking one surprise blow after another when the enemy forces were divided.

During the next few years, the pioneers of the New World struggled against incredible odds. Supplies were limited and once-friendly Indians turned hostile. The untimely death of Menéndez in 1574 almost became the coup de grace for the tiny community as officials in Spain debated its future. Finally swayed by the settlement's importance as a deterrent to enemy occupation of Florida and as a haven on the shipping route between the Caribbean and Spain, the crown subsidized the colony of St. Augustine through the viceroy of New Spain (Mexico).

The harbor town grew stronger under the new system, and by its twenty-first year it consisted of a council house, church, stores, and homes for the three hundred inhabitants. The old log fort was rapidly decaying when news arrived that the notorious corsair, Sir Francis Drake, was plundering Spanish colonies in the Caribbean. A new wooden fort was hastily constructed during the early months of 1586, but was no defense against the overwhelming English force. Only smoking ashes remained when the Spaniards came from the forest to watch the white sails disappear over the horizon—and to begin rebuilding.

An essential ingredient in colonization was conversion of the natives to Christianity. Early attempts by the Jesuit Order had been thwarted by Indian hostility, and the few Franciscans present during the 1570s also made little progress. One of the structures erected after Drake's attack was a new monastery to house other friars sent from Spain to bolster the missionary effort. By 1595 the Franciscans had saved 1,500 souls; Bishop Altamirano, visiting in 1606, counted two thousand Indian converts. To officials in Spain, the Christian mission enhanced the value of the struggling community that so often faced abandonment by the mother country.

It was during the last decade of the sixteenth century that the garrison town began to take shape. The town plan followed the specifications issued by the Spanish king for all colonies—a central plaza with major thoroughfares radiating from it. An official residence for the governor was erected on the west end of the plaza, and the capital city continued to survive. Even the devastating fire of 1599 and hurricane of the same year failed to quell its spirit.

As St. Augustine reached its centennial, the English were busily colonizing the continent north of the Florida peninsula. Pleas for aid in strengthening the garrison went unheeded by Spanish authorities, leaving the town defenseless in 1668 when the English pirate Robert Searles (alias Davis) sacked the city, killing and injuring numerous inhabitants.

Finally, after the English colony of Charleston, South Carolina, was founded in 1670, the need for stronger fortification was recognized, and Queen Regent Marianna authorized construction of a stone fort. The Castillo de San Marcos, begun in 1672, reached completion by 1695. As the massive gray walls received finishing touches, private citizens were granted permission to use the valuable building material. Coquina (shellstone) quarried on Anastasia Island formed the substantial walls of many new houses. Around this time the Franciscan monks also received a permanent shelter built of this stone.

Hardly were the bastion walls in place when the town was forced to prove its defensibility. Carolina Governor James Moore led a force of six hundred men against the Spanish garrison town. For two months the siege continued, creating extensive damage within the city. The fort held, however, and Moore retreated, leaving the citadel intact but the town in ruins. No buildings, save a few coquina walls, withstood the English torch.

Again the populace rallied and rebuilt the

Ponce de León has overlooked the ancient city since 1923, when Dr. Andrew Anderson unveiled this statue, a replica of the monument in San Juan, Puerto Rico. At the time of this mid-1920s photograph, the St. Johns Electric Company trolleys still carried passengers across the wooden bridge to Anastasia Island. Photograph from the St. Augustine Historical Society.

power and land. St. Augustine would not fall to enemy gun; rather the fate of the garrison town would be determined by the stroke of a pen.

Florida's First Families

The oldest documented family in the nation's oldest city is the Solana family, a claim verified by the document of marriage and veiling of Vincent Solana and Maria Visente in 1594. The Solana family prospered in the early years of Spanish St. Augustine with recorded births and baptisms and an unbroken line of marriage records of the numerous descendants of Vincent and Maria.

When Spanish rule ended, the exodus of citizens left only eight men remaining in an official capacity. Most of these disappeared from the records during the British period (1763-83), but Manuel Solana, direct descendant of Vincent, was an active part of the changing community. He married twice, first to Mary Mitchell of London, England, and later to Minorcan Maria Masters (Maestre) in 1781. Manuel and Mary's children were: Philipe (died in infancy), Lorenzo, and Maria Dolores. Eleven offspring resulted from the union of Manuel and Maria Masters. Certainly thirteen children were a substantial number to maintain the Solana line through the second Spanish period (1784-1821) and into United States possession.

Second in age is the Alvarez-Sánchez family, with documentation in 1602 of Diego Alvarez's marriage to Elena Gonzáles. In 1714 descendants of this family united with the Sánchez de Ortegosa family through the marriage of Diego and Elena's great-great-granddaughter, Juana Theodora Pérez to José Sánchez de Ortegosa.

A third family producing descentants in the ancient city is the Arsián-Alvarez-Gonzáles family. Documentation for the Alvarez family dates from 1597; the Arsián family records a marriage in 1623. The families united when Captain Antonio Rodríguez Arsián married an Alvarez descendant in 1685. The Gonzáles family is added through Juan Gonzáles, Sr., an Arsián descendant who married his fourth cousin of the Alvarez line. This family blended with the Oliveros in 1823.

Above:
Dr. Ansel Brush Philips (1844-1911) was born at Redbank in South Jacksonville, but spent his adult life in St. Augustine as a dentist and the husband of Maria Anita Solana. Philips Highway in Jacksonville was named for Ansel's father, Albert Gallatin Philips. Photograph courtesy of Earl. L. "Ike" Masters.

Above right:
Maria Anita Solana (1841-1898) married Ansel Brush Philips in 1868. The Philipses lived on the corner of Bay Street and Cathedral where the American Legion Building (Hamblen home) now stands. Photograph courtesy of Earl L. "Ike" Masters.

Miss Hattie Sanchez rocks on the porch of the house in Spuds built in 1883 by her father, Henry. She was eighty-seven years old at the time of the photograph in 1975. Photograph courtesy of St. Ambrose Parish.

Henry Sanchez plays his fiddle in front of his corn house in Spuds in the early 1880s. Photograph courtesy of St. Ambrose Parish.

"Miss Mena" Oliveros represented the Catholic Daughters at a conference in 1978; her age was ninety-six. Mena Oliveros is a descendant of the first Spanish period family of Arsián-Alvarez-Gonzáles, a link formed by the marriage in 1823 of Fernanda Gonzáles and Mena's great-grandfather, Bartolome Oliveros. Photograph courtesy of Mena Oliveros.

Far left:
Dennis Solana, in an early 1900s photograph, is one of twelve children born to Philip and Mary Louise Masters Solana. Photograph courtesy of Louis Solana.

Left:
Lottie Solana Andreu around 1906. Photograph courtesy of Louis Solana.

Charlotte Street looking north across Treasury Street before the turn of the century. The one-story coquina structure on the right exemplifies St. Augustine houses of the first Spanish occupation. The Puente map lists it as the residence of Don Juan de Mata Pérez. Although altered considerably over the years, the extant structure has retained the original walls and arches. Photograph courtesy of Mary La Verne Peck.

Far left:
This 1880s garden view shows the north addition of the Oldest House with the porch extending from the earlier south side rooms. Photograph from the St. Augustine Historical Society.

Left:
Some extraordinary changes occurred while the Oldest House was owned by the C. P. Carver family. Mary E. Carver purchased the house in 1884, and, with her husband, Charles, a local dentist, modified the house inside and out. The round masonry tower was constructed on the northeast corner. Dormers were added as well as roof-shelters over the windows and entrances. The Carvers used woodwork and colored glass from the old Presbyterian church to panel the coquina walls and to decorate windows. The Carvers were the first to show the house for a fee. James W. Henderson purchased the house from the Carvers and continued to use it as a showplace. He added a garage apartment to the west end before selling to the South Beach Alligator Farm and Museum of Curios. In 1918 the St. Augustine Historical Society purchased the house, restoring it to its present state in 1960. Photograph from the St. Augustine Historical Society.

Left:
The Oldest House has been restored by the Historical Society to its eighteenth-century appearance. Archeological research indicates continuous occupation of the site from the early 1600s. Documentation in 1727 gives evidence of residency by Tomas Gonzales y Hernandez, a Canary Islander who, with his wife, Francisca de Guevarra, lived in the St. Francis Street house until British occupation of St. Augustine. After the structure had been vacant for ten years, Major Joseph Peavett bought the property from Jesse Fish, adding portions of the upper story and making other improvements. The British officer died in 1786, and Spanish authorities sold the property in public sale to Geronimo Alvarez. Alvarez, a native of Spain, was a prominent citizen serving as Alcalde Mayor. *The house was later conveyed to Alvarez's son, Antonio, himself influential in local politics. The Alvarez family remained after the change of flags in 1821, the property never leaving possession of the family until 1882. Photograph from the St. Augustine Historical Society.*

The Oldest House

The house on St. Francis Street known as the Oldest House has experienced numerous structural modifications exemplifying the evolution from "common plan" to "St. Augustine plan," typical of many ancient city residences. It began as a one- or two-room masonry structure with an upper story over these rooms appearing sometime before 1788. Further additions were made by adding rooms on the north side, both upper and lower stories. A porch with an easterly exposure extends from the south section of the house.

Numerous buildings arose in this fashion, often with spacious loggias as an integral part of the plan. Overhanging balconies sprouted above the streets, frequently changing appearance with each new owner. Wings were added (and sometimes removed), and with the British came the addition of fireplaces and chimneys. Houses were built to accommodate the Florida climate; south and east exposures were common, as were thick masonry walls which provided insulation from the summer heat and protection from the winter chill.

The spacious loggia of the Don Pedro Horruytiner House typifies several architectural aspects popular in early St. Augustine structures. The loggia opens into the side yard, not onto the street, and has a southern exposure since south or east openings permit optimal comfort during summer heat or winter winds. The outdoor stairway of tabby was common during the first Spanish and British periods and was generally set back from the main porch area to afford protection from the elements. Note the individual design of each interior arch. This 1914 photo was taken during occupancy by the Lindsley family. Dr. Horace E. Lindsley purchased the structure in 1896, and it remained in possession of the family until 1977. Photograph courtesy of James S. Lindsley.

The Arrivas house is pictured here around 1870. It receives its name from the first documented owner, Don Raimundo de Arrivas, an infantry lieutenant of the first Spanish period who lived with his wife, Ursula Avero, and their children in the coquina structure around 1748-64. At the close of the British period his son, Don Tadeo de Arrivas, returned to St. Augustine as clerk of the Royal Treasury and reclaimed the house. He sold the property after his return to Cuba when Spain again relinquished possession of Florida. The house has been restored to the early Territorial period appearance and contains a silversmith shop on the first floor. Photograph from the Historic St. Augustine Preservation Board.

This 1890s photo shows the porch of the St. George Hotel with the residence of Dr. Horace E. Lindsley in the background at right and his offices in the small building on the left. The tall Lyon Building rises above the house, which bears the Horruytiner name for its original occupant of the First Spanish period. Two members of the Horruytiner family were governors during the time, and the family was evidently wealthy and prominent within the community. Apparently the walls of the coquina structure endured after Moore's 1702 siege, for Lorenzo Horruytiner petitioned the government for four hundred pesos to repair fire damage. Photograph from the St. Augustine Historical Society.

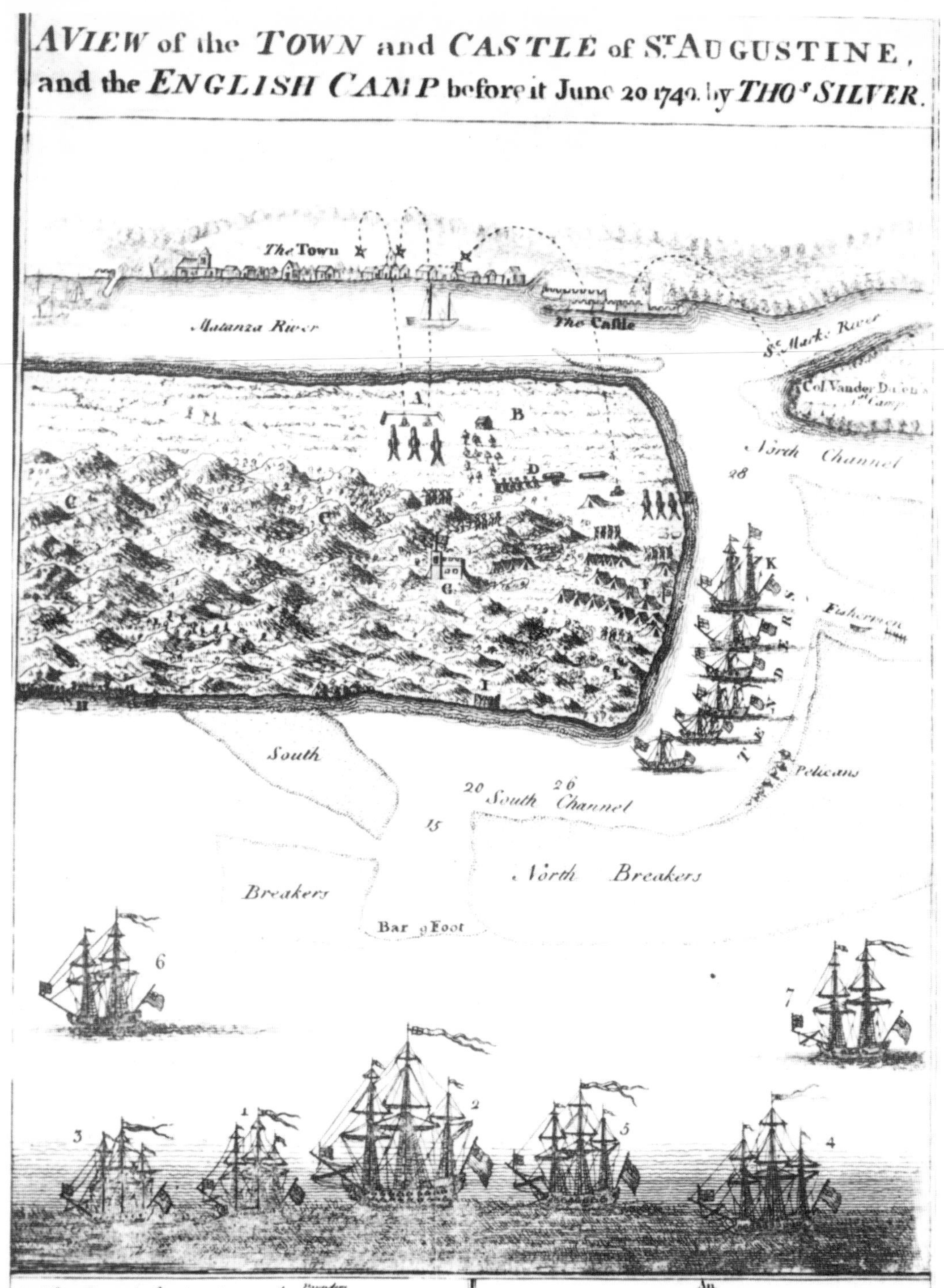

The attack by General James Oglethorpe was one of the many tragedies and hardships endured by settlers of the little harbor town; his invasion, however, was unsuccessful. St. Augustine's strong land defense prevented attack on foot. When the English ships were unable to pass through the narrow inlet, Oglethorpe was forced to bombard the city from a point on Anastasia Island (now Davis Shores). Even his relentless harassment did little damage to his target, the fort, or the town. Map from Florida Photographic Archives, Strozier Library, F.S.U.

To make the old Castillo an effective unit in the United States coastal defense system, army engineers built a new water battery, right, in 1842. As this view shows, however, the guns were gone by the 1870s; the Confederates moved them elsewhere at the outbreak of the Civil War. The small structure, center, is a furnace for heating cannon balls red hot to burn enemy targets. From Florida Photographic Archives, Strozier Library, F.S.U.

Construction of the Castillo de San Marcos was essential to the survival of the tiny military outpost of St. Augustine. For years wooden forts served as defense centers, but proved inadequate protection. The English first found St. Augustine's Achilles' heel; in 1586 Sir Francis Drake's fleet of twenty ships and two thousand men sacked and burned the town. Rebuilt from ashes, the struggling settlement was anxiously awaiting aid from the mother country when, in 1668, the English pirate Robert Searles (alias Davis) attacked the fort and plundered the town. Meanwhile, the threat of English colonization in the north significantly increased. The pirate attack coupled with the 1670 colonization of Charleston prompted Queen Mariana to authorize a stone fortification for St. Augustine. Construction began in 1672. Coquina (shellstone) was quarried on Anastasia Island, and slowly the impenetrable walls rose, reaching completion in 1695. Photograph by Victor Rahner; from the National Park Service.

Fort Matanzas received face lifts in 1916 and in the 1920s. The tower portion was first to be repaired, and the gun deck and sentry box were restored after the fort became a national monument in 1924. The fort has been solely administered by the National Park Service since 1935. Photograph from the St. Augustine Historical Society.

The walls of Fort Matanzas arose in 1742 to protect St. Augustine from enemy encroachment via the inland waterway. Photographed in 1913, the ruins stand as a grim reminder of the neglect of the second Spanish period, when the fortress fell into disrepair. The historical significance of the inlet site is increased by the gruesome event which took place across the river 174 years prior to completion of the masonry walls. While Menendez and French Huguenot Jean Ribault vied for control of the Florida coast in 1565, Ribault's fleet was shipwrecked in a storm. The Frenchmen attempted to reach Fort Caroline by foot. One group approached a spot fourteen miles south of St. Augustine when Menendez overtook them. More than one hundred men surrendered to Menendez, crossed the river, and met death. Ribault arrived twelve days later with the remainder of his crew. They, too, encountered Spanish swords, not mercy, and the inlet earned its name — Matanzas is the Spanish word for slaughter. From the Florida Photographic Archives, Strozier Library, F.S.U.

Tourists explored the fascinating fortress long before it became a national monument in 1924. From Florida Photographic Archives, Strozier Library, F.S.U.

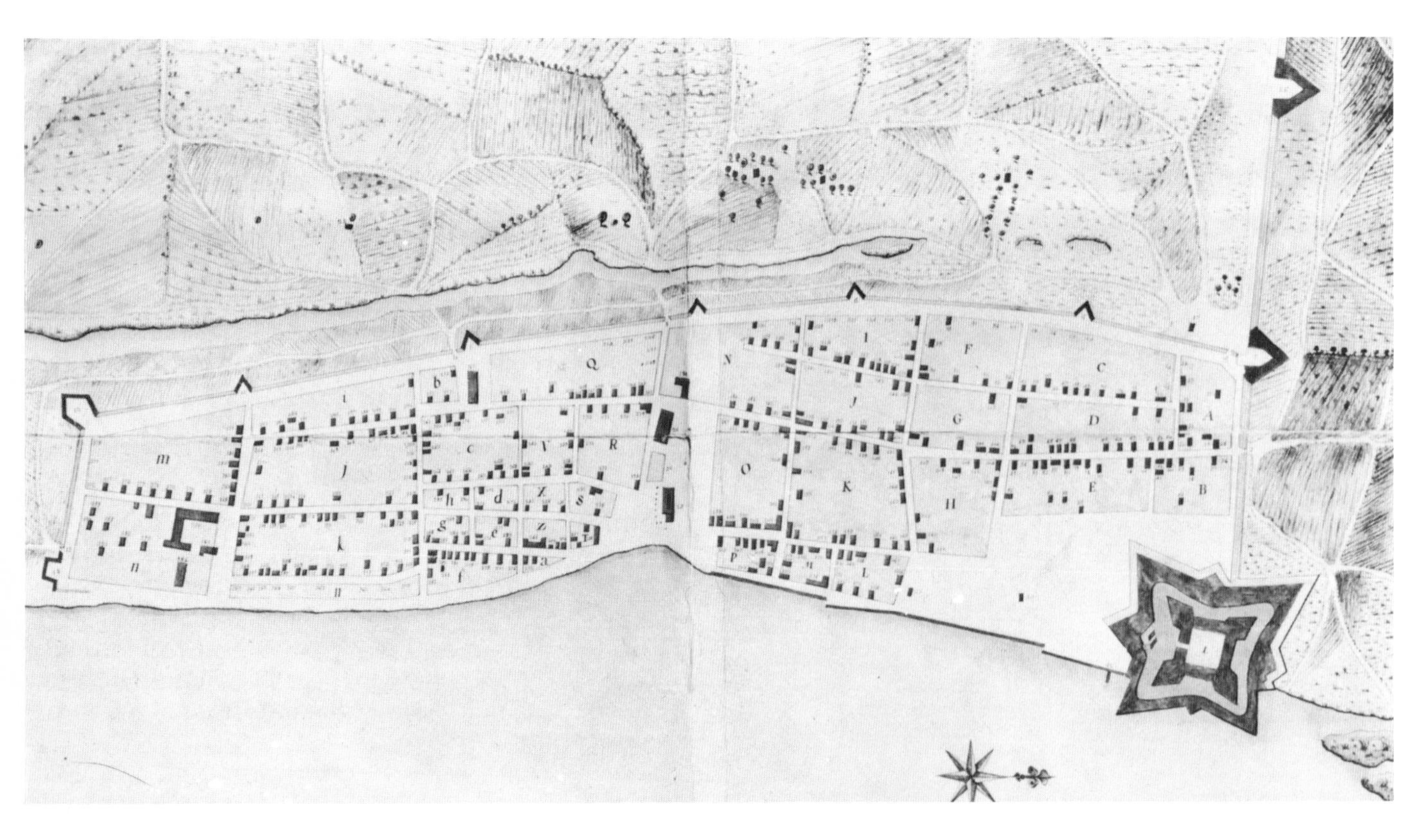

Don Juan Josef Elixio de la Puente was a wealthy Spaniard appointed by the king to dispose of Spanish property at the outset of the British period (1763-83). The map bearing his name was drawn in 1764 and is indispensable in determining building locations and property ownership of the first Spanish period. The plaza is situated in the center of town, between blocks R and O. The darkened areas designate a guard house (closest to the water), a privately owned lot, and church property. The darkened right angle in block N is the governor's residence. King Street extends from the bayfront to the western boundary, passing between blocks Q and N. The Castillo de San Marcos dominates the northeast corner, bottom right of the map. St. George Street runs the length of the town beginning at the City Gate, the northern boundary to the right of the map, and ending at St. Francis Street just north of block M and N, left on the map. St. Francis Barracks is located in the upper right corner of block N. A later map, drawn in 1788 by the Spanish royal engineer, Mariano de la Rocque, substantiates the Puente map and gives a detailed picture of changes during the British decades. Drawing from the Historic St. Augustine Preservation Board.

Chapter Two

The British Decades: 1763-1784

The British are represented in this 1920s Ponce de Leon parade down St. George Street. Photograph by H. M. Tucker; courtesy of Howard Hanson.

The devastating news announced in March 1763 shocked St. Augustine citizens far more than if enemy fire had suddenly exploded from across the harbor; Spain had ceded Florida to England in exchange for occupied Havana and other territorial possessions of value to Spain. Spanish citizens were required to evacuate the city or declare loyalty to the British crown. Soon families boarded ships bound for Cuba and the West Indies, taking with them whatever possessions could fit aboard the overloaded vessels. Of the slightly more than three thousand inhabitants, only eight remained—each acting in an official capacity as mediator for the rival countries.

At first the somnolent town waited quietly, occupied only by a small staff of Englishmen and a few soldiers. Gradually a small number of families trickled in, and land speculators visited the old city to consider investment in the strange new territory. Despite size and appearance, the ancient city held a position of importance. The British divided the new possession into two provinces of East and West Florida, with Pensacola capital of the western portion and St. Augustine the eastern capital.

By August 1764 the first governor, Colonel James Grant, arrived, and the two-hundred-year-old Spanish town began to acquire a British veneer. Soldiers moved into the commodious friary, adding a three-story wooden barracks on adjacent property. The name of the Castillo de San Marcos was anglicized to Fort Saint Marks. Governor Grant moved into the residence at the west end of the plaza, remodeling the structure and adding a coach house, stables, and laundry.

The Spanish church south of the plaza was converted to an Anglican house of prayer with a new steeple modifying the skyline and bells summoning worshipers to service. The first Anglican minister, John Forbes, soon found his way into politics, becoming an influential leader and wealthy landowner as he led his flock through two decades of Protestantism.

The hospital near the plaza became the jail, and the bishop's house beside the governor's residence was used as the state house. The little

This statue commemorating Minorcan priest Father Pedro Camps was dedicated in 1975 in the Cathedral courtyard. Unveiling the statue is Xavier L. Pellicer, co-donor with Fernando A. Rubio, (seated in inset). Doctor Rubio, a native Minorcan who has contributed generously to the memory of the Minorcans of the New Smyrna colony, operates a wholesale drug company in over twenty countries. His interest in his countrymen and the bond with their Minorcan descendants frequently brings him to St. Augustine. Photographs courtesy of Xavier L. Pellicer.

"Dutch Church" outside the city limits was razed, having previously served as both an Indian mission and a house of worship for the "deutch" colonists from Switzerland. As families moved into the vacant houses, they adapted the residences to accommodate their needs. Fireplaces were built and second-story rooms were added to many coquina structures consisting of only ground level space. Balconies on the larger houses protruded over the streets, a mute reminder of the Spanish heritage of the past. The sale of the residences was often administered by Jesse Fish, the Englishman who had lived in St. Augustine since 1736, and with whom much property had been left in trust.

During the ensuing years the British began exporting indigo, oranges, lumber, and naval stores. One of the larger landowners, Lieutenant Governor John Moultrie, maintained residency both on his plantation (Bella Vista, south of town) and in his house near the plaza. Moultrie temporarily succeeded Grant as governor when Grant returned to England in 1771.

In order to colonize new territories, governments frequently issued land grants to prospective settlers, a practice followed by England while striving to develop the new possession. One such grant was secured by Dr. Andrew Turnbull and associates, who acquired 100,000 acres of land located at Mosquito Inlet, approximately eighty miles south of St. Augustine. Naming the location New Smyrna for his Greek wife's birthplace, Turnbull set about the task of recruiting colonists for the proposed indigo plantation. His preference was for settlers of Greek nationality who were farmers by profession and followed an Orthodox faith, and he successfully enticed about two hundred adventurers from his wife's homeland, taking them to the British-held port of Mahon, Minorca, while he and his partners, Sir William Duncan and Sir Richard Temple, searched for additional colonists. Several Italian families joined them, but the majority of recruits were obtained from Minorca. The small Balaric island had suffered three years of famine, and the poverty-stricken farmers and fishermen were grateful for this unexpected opportunity; the conditions of indentured service promised freedom from obligation and a parcel of land after a period of approximately seven years of work. Turnbull purchased five hundred Negroes for use as slave labor on the plantation. A ship carrying the slaves sailed from Africa about the same time the colonists left Minorca, but it never reached its destination; the ship sank, taking its human cargo to the bottom of the sea — an omen for the ill-fated colony.

Approximately 1,400 Mediterraneans sailed for Florida in March 1768. Before the eight ships arrived in the new land, 148 passengers died, many from starvation. Turnbull had underestimated the difficulty of providing for such a large number of people, an error which was intensified after their landing in New Smyrna. The colony was beset by problems of inadequate shelter and food. Three hundred died the first winter.

The departure of Governor Grant in 1771 came as a blow to Turnbull. As a supporter of the project, Grant had been an important ally. Now, with the colonists rebelling against the intolerable conditions within the settlement, Turnbull faced careful scrutiny by the new governor, Patrick Tonyn, an ardent English Loyalist who took office in East Florida in 1774.

While Turnbull was defending himself in England, the six hundred remaining colonists requested protection from the sympathetic governor. In 1777 they fled the tyranny of servitude. Led by Francisco Pellicer, several hundred settlers marched along King's Road to the safety of St. Augustine, settling initially on land provided by Governor Tonyn north of the City Gate. Those who remained to harvest the crops arrived in November, a group which included the beloved priest, Father Pedro Camps.

As the New Smyrna emigrants settled into a peaceful existence, the harsh winds of revolutionary war continued to blow throughout the English colonies. Loyal to the crown, St. Augustine became a haven for those escaping the zeal of

IN MEMORY OF
FATHER PEDRO CAMPS
THE SPIRITUAL LEADER OF THE
MINORCAN COLONY
THIS STATUE PRESENTED TO
REVEREND PAUL F.
BISHOP OF ST. AUGUSTINE BY
A. RUBIO OF
AND
APRIL 24, 1975
IN COMMEMORATION OF THE
TWO HUNDRETH ANNIVERSARY

Ernest Oliveros (1857-1942) was a sports enthusiast who loved his race horses and fighting gamecocks. An Oliveros ancestor, Sebastian, was a native of Corsica who appears in Florida history about the time of the New Smyrna colony. Records do not show that he was a member of that group; however, in 1795 he married a Minorcan girl, Catalina Usina. Photograph courtesy of Mena Oliveros.

American patriots. In 1740, forty such patriots were imprisoned in the walled city. Three were signers of the Declaration of Independence—Edward Rutledge, Arthur Middleton, and Thomas Heyward, Jr. As the Revolution was resolved, more Loyalists fled to East Florida, its population reaching seventeen thousand in 1781-82. The first newspaper, the *East Florida Gazette*, was printed at this time, and Governor Tonyn called the first legislative assembly. Prosperity was short-lived, however, for in April 1783 Governor Tonyn announced that England had ceded the Floridas and Minorca back to Spain in order to retain Gibraltar and other territories. The evacuation was slow and painful, leaving only the New Smyrna emigrants undisturbed by the change in government.

Descendants of the New Smyrna Colony

The Minorcan story does not end with the colonists' migration to St. Augustine in 1777. Rather, the entry into the city marks an epoch in the development of the vulnerable little town. Within a few years, the British were compelled to return the town to Spanish rule. For the second time, almost an entire population evacuated the city, but 460 Minorcans, Italians, and Greeks remained to greet the Spanish governor in 1784, and for almost forty years they lived in an atmosphere akin to their own Mediterranean backgrounds.

However, 1821 brought further change; lives were again disrupted when Florida became a United States territory. Again, the bulk of St. Augustine's remaining citizens consisted of members of the colony or their descendants. The descendants pictured here represent a few of the families that trace their origin in this country to the New Smyrna colony. A list of forty-eight family names is engraved on a tablet at the foot of the Father Camps memorial statue.

Dionecia Masters (1846-1939), daughter of Antonio Juan Fernando Masters and Matilda Pinal, is of a lineage begun in Florida by Antonio Bartolome de Mestre and his wife, Antonia Rogero. This couple came from Minorca with four children. The oldest, Pedro, married Maria Andreu and produced twelve offspring. Members of the Masters family married Solana descendants, thus creating a link between the first Spanish and British periods of the city's history. Photograph courtesy of Earl L. "Ike" Masters.

Raymond F. Sabate (1862-c.1945) is remembered for his work as deputy sheriff from 1901 to 1922 under sheriffs Perry and Boyce. His wife, Henrietta de Mier, brought the Spanish heritage to the lineage carried by their descendants. Photograph from the St. Augustine Historical Society.

Left to right: Katherine Masters Braddock, Ignacio Ortagus, and Emma Cubbedge Ortagus stand beside a Model-T Ford. Photograph courtesy of Gaby Lee (Mrs. Charles R.) Usina.

Catherine Urbana Pellicer sits with her parents, Elmanuel Aguiar Pellicer and Bertha Helen Canova Pellicer, in 1909. The child's heritage includes Minorcan names such as Andreu, Caules, Rogero, Ponz, Masters, Villalonga, and Riola. A Greek ancestry comes from the Cercopoly family, Italian from Pacetti, and Spanish through the Noda and Bravo names. Photograph courtesy of Geraldine Rowe Maguire.

Belva Andreu in 1905. The Andreu (Andrew) family traces a Florida heritage from Juan Andreu II and Maria Angela Caules, who married in Minorca in 1737, and later sailed to Mosquito Inlet with their children. Photograph courtesy of Earl L. "Ike" Masters.

Bishop Dominic Manucy (1823-85) provides the background for an interesting and inspirational account of two Minorcan descendants. Dominic was the son of Maria Lorenzo and Pedro Manucy. Before Dominic was a year old, the Manucys accepted the infant Anthony Domingo Pellicer into their home. The baby was one of a set of twins born to Francisco Pellicer, Jr., and Margarita Joaneda, who died in childbirth. The two children were blood cousins, for Anthony Domingo's grandmother, Juana Villa Pellicer, and Dominic's grandmother, Maria Villa Lorenzo, were sisters. The boys were reared together in the native Minorcan style with a solid Catholic upbringing shaping their values. As teenagers they attended Bishop Portier's school in Spring Hill, Alabama, studying together until their ordination in 1850. Dominic Manucy's first assignment was parish priest in Pensacola, Florida; his cousin became pastor of St. Peter's Church, Montgomery, Alabama. Both were recognized in 1874 for their dedicated service when Domingo Pellicer was named first Bishop of San Antonio, Texas, and Father Manucy was appointed first Vicar Apostolic of Brownsville, Texas. Dominic remained in that position until he was named Bishop of Mobile in 1884, a year before a serious illness claimed his life. Photograph courtesy of Texas Catholic Archives.

Bishop Anthony Domingo Pellicer (1824-1880) was appointed first Bishop of San Antonio in 1874. He descends from Francisco Pellicer, the chosen leader of the colonists who elected to abandon New Smyrna. Francisco, a master carpenter, established himself rapidly and prosperously in St. Augustine. Francisco, Jr., was one of the many children born to his second wife, Juana Villa. It was the wife of Francisco, Jr., who died shortly after giving birth to Anthony Domingo and his twin. As Bishop in Texas, Anthony Domingo demonstrated an extensive interest in education and the problems of orphaned children. Photograph courtesy of Xavier L. Pellicer.

The Triay and Weedman families, around Elkton, circa 1910. Left to right: three brothers, Paul, Edward (beside the woman), and Eugene Weedman; Mae Triay wears the white blouse and Tanti Triay Masters, a sister of Mae, stands on the right. The child at right is Leo, the child at left, Arnold; both are children of Tanti and Eulesus Masters. The Triay family traces its roots to Juan Triay and his wife, Maria (maiden name also Triay). They arrived with the Turnbull group, bringing two teenage sons, Francisco and Juan, Jr. Photograph courtesy of Charley Sanchez.

Three Ortagus brothers are pictured with a friend, Posey Foster, standing at left. Seated are Henry, left, and Herman, with Ernie in back, right. Photograph courtesy of Gaby Lee (Mrs. Charles R.) Usina.

Louis Ortagus represented the Sampson area of St. Johns county as a member of the county commission in the 1920s. The Ortagus (originally Ortega) family traces its Florida heritage to Ignacio and Ana Ortega, who brought their twelve-year-old son Lazaro to New Smyrna. Photograph courtesy of Gaby Lee (Mrs. Charles R.) Usina.

The Rogero family stop their car (a 1911-12, EMF Roadster) on Aviles Street: Francis Herbert Rogero, Sr., his wife, Rosa Rogero, and children Herbert, Jr., left, and Ione. Ione was known in the community as Sister Mary Herbert, a teacher and principal of St. Joseph's Academy. Photograph courtesy of Albert Rogero.

Rudolph Pomar operated this grocery store in the Mallette Building located on San Marco Avenue between Cincinnati Avenue and Hope Street. Jose Pomar came to New Smyrna with his wife, Juana Llina, and one-year-old son, Juan. Jose apparently did not survive the ordeal at Mosquito Inlet, but ten-year-old Juan accompanied his mother to St. Augustine. He later married Martina Hernandez, a child of the colony. Photograph courtesy of Ellie Shepherd (Mrs. Roscoe) Pomar.

Left:
Fernanda Capo Ximenez (1846-1936) was celebrating her 89th birthday when this photograph was taken. Her parents were Juan Capo (grandson of Juan Capo of New Smyrna) and Maria Felani (Fallany or Falleni). A daughter, Catherine, carried this lineage and added another Minorcan name through marriage to James L. Ponce. Their son, James V. Ponce, married Geronima Solana, giving their descendants a heritage from both the first Spanish and British periods of St. Augustine's history. Photograph courtesy of James A. Ponce, Sr.

Right:
Clarence Pappy in his World War I uniform. Gaspar Papi was of Greek origin and made his way to Florida through Turnbull's colony. He was the only known native of Smyrna, the city for which the colony was named. Photograph courtesy of Eulalia Walker Langston Compton.

A Capo family photo in 1898. Left to right, standing: Leon, Walton, Pauline, Clarence, Edna; seated: Paul holding Edmund, Eunice, and Ellen holding Cecil. Photograph courtesy of Eunice Banta Bowen.

Margarita Antonia Capo (1847-1923) was seventeen years old when Roscoe Perry was assigned to Fort Marion with the 17th Connecticut Regiment. St. Augustine had been occupied by Union troops since March 1862, and sentiments of the townfolk were both diverse and deep as the soldiers walked the ancient city streets. Roscoe Perry saw the young girl of Minorcan descent and courted her until military orders sent him home to be mustered out of the army. He returned the following year, however, and they married in October 1865. The couple's first home was on St. George Street in the house which is now the Museum of Yesterday's Toys. Perry's initial business venture in the city was a grocery store operated from that building. Photograph courtesy of Eleanor Philips Barnes.

Mary Lawler Small sits with her granddaughter, Mary Alice Mickler (later Masters). Mrs. Small, the great-granddaughter of Gaspar Papi, carried a heritage that included both the Papi (Greek) and Peso de Burgo (Corsican) lineages. Photograph courtesy of Mary Alice Mickler Masters.

Frank Andreu Usina stands on Corbett's Dock on the bayfront around 1920. The Usina name, often spelled Alzina or Alcina, comes from the New Smyrna colonist Antonio Usina, who married Catalina Mell in 1770. Their twins, Maria and Catalina, and a son, Bartolome Miguel, were born before the family arrived in St. Augustine from Mosquito Inlet. After the death of Catalina Mell, Antonio married Rafaela Capo, a Minorcan of the colony. Photograph courtesy of Mary (Mrs. Francis) Usina.

Domingo Pedro Pacetti, Sr. (1828-92), photographed circa 1865. The Pacetti (Paxety) family from Italy found its way to Florida through Andreas Paxety, who came to New Smyrna with his first wife, Gertrude Pons. In 1785 he married Maria Rosario Castel. Children of these unions married into the families of Capo, Lopez, and Triay, creating bonds within those family units. Photograph courtesy of Lorna Pacett Ortagus.

Bartolo Thomas Genovar (1846-1945) and Mary Louise Gomez (1851-1945) pose for their wedding picture in June 1872. Bartolo's ancestor Juan Genovar arrived in New Smyrna with a four-year-old son, Francisco Juan. In 1797, comfortably settled in St. Augustine, Francisco married Antonia Peregri, daughter of Bartolome Peregri and Juana Hernandez, perpetuating the Genovar name. Of Spanish descent, Mary Louise's allied families include Alvarez, Mendez, Norman, Ribas, and Tejeda. Her father, John Gomez, explored much of Florida's untamed terrotory and possessed an extensive land grant. Bartolo and Mary Louise began married life in the large Bay Street house which is now the Chart House restaurant. From there they moved to 20 Bay Street, later the Elks Club headquarters before the structure was razed. Photograph courtesy of Eugenia Y. Genovar.

Antonia Hernandez Pacetti (1830-1909) was the granddaughter of Brigadier General Joseph Hernandez. As the wife of Domingo Pacetti she lived a difficult existence in "the country," now Pacetti Road in Bakersville. A bit of oral history relates an incident during the Civil War when Antonia hid her husband in a baby crib to protect him from Union capture. Photograph courtesy of Lorna Pacetti Ortagus.

The Rogero family celebrate Christmas in 1919 in the Grove Avenue home. Left to right, back row: Elmo (Irene Lopez) Rogero, Mrs. Francis Herbert Rogero (Rosa), Catherine Rogero, Marea Rogero, Mrs. William (Lorenza) Schmidt; seated on porch: Francis Emanuel Rogero and wife, Mary Masters Rogero; top steps: Marie Schmidt, Wilma Rogero, Alma Rogero, Eva Mae Rogero, Ambrosina Brown with baby Claire, Burke Rogero (standing); middle steps: Ione Rogero, Louise Rogero, Helen Schmidt, E.J. Rogero, Jr., William Schmidt (standing); bottom steps: Francis Herbert Rogero, Jr., Anita Brown, Faustina Rogero, Michael James Rogero, Roger Brown, Edgar Brown (standing). Photograph courtesy of Albert Rogero.

Mark Manucy (1842-97) married Evalina Masters in 1866. Here he holds their granddaughter, Enis. Mark pursued a vocation of carpentry as did his father, Phillip. He was elected city alderman in 1879 Photograph courtesy of Albert C. Manucy.

Evalina Masters Manucy (1840-1933) holds her great-grandson, John Prescott Whitney, Jr., in this 1922 photograph. In addition to the Masters and Manucy names, the baby claims a lineage which includes the names of Pomar, Capo, and Mickler. Photograph courtesy of Annie Masters.

The child Eleanor Philips grew to love and cherish the valuable heritage of the nation's oldest city. Through her efforts, scores of families and individuals now possess documented evidence of their ancestory. Eleanor Philips Barnes' sense of history led to the development of the traditional Easter Festival's Royal Family. Photograph courtesy of Margaret Manford.

Emily Masters pauses in front of the Market Place with her bicycle, circa 1898. Photograph courtesy of St. Ambrose Parish.

Richard Leonardi, now the owner of a jewelry store, holds the hand of younger brother Donald, around 1912. The first Leonardi in Florida was Roque, born about 1742 in Nodena, Italy. He came with his wife, Esperanza Moll (or Valle), who gave birth to two daughters while in the colony. Roque married a second time in 1773, and he and his wife, Agueda Coll, became parents of eleven offspring. Photograph courtesy of Mr. and Mrs. Wallace Leonardi.

General Stephen Vincent Benet (1827-1895) was the son of Pedro Benet and Juana Hernandez Benet. After receiving a degree from the University of Georgia, the eighteen-year-old became Florida's first appointee to West Point Military Academy. He was the youngest brigadier general of his time, achieving the rank in 1874, after a distinguished career which included service to the Union during the Civil War. It was his son, James Walker Benet, who fathered the famous literary geniuses Stephen Vincent, William Rose, and Laura Benet. Photograph from the St. Augustine Historical Society.

The Avero House on St. George Street now contains the St. Photios Shrine commemorating Greek immigrants of the New Smyrna colony. The Avero House takes its name from the first period Spanish family who owned and built on this lot. They vacated the coquina structure when they departed for Cuba in 1763. In 1777 British Governor Tonyn gave the residence to Father Pedro Camps, an act demonstrating freedom of religion not only to the Catholics who migrated to St. Augustine from New Smyrna, but also to the Greeks within the colony. The names of Gianopoli, Cosafacis, and Papi represent some of the surviving colonists of Greek descent. Desiring a place of worship, they, too, found sanctuary within the walls of the Avero House. Although some of the Greeks from Corsica were Catholics, others may have followed their native religion. Those who married Catholics possibly worshipped with their wives in the same building with their Greek compatriots. Through the work of Olga and George Fotiou, Despina and Thomas Xynides, Jerry and Steve Sarres, Stella and James Kalivas, and Martha and Spiras Zappatos, the house now owned by the Greek Orthodox Church—and a newly constructed Orthodox Chapel—will perpetuate the memory of early Greek settlers. The shrine is named St. Photios for one of the great patriarchs, teachers, and missionary saints of their faith. Photograph from the St. Augustine Historical Society.

The Llambias House itself is a chapter in the Minorcan story. Owned at one time by Nicholas Turnbull, the son of Dr. Andrew Turnbull, the house became the property of Minorcans and their descendants beginning with the purchase in 1795 by Juan Andreu, Sr. Peter and Joseph Manucy were the next owners, selling the structure in 1854 to Joseph and Catalina Usina Llambias. Several Llambias children were born in the house. In 1889 Ada Llambias married Edward Reyes and made the house home to three Reyes children born there. This sketch of the St. Francis Street house was drawn by Edith Oliver, the wife of R. J. Oliver, operator of a grocery store on Charlotte Street around the turn of the century. Erected prior to 1763, the structure underwent numerous additions and modifications over the decades. Restoration was completed in 1954, preserving its late eighteenth-century appearance. Drawing courtesy of Antonica Piet.

Charles E. "Ted" Pellicer watches the assembly of a chair for the Llambias House. The furniture was fashioned in Mahon, Minorca, and given as a gift by Fernando A. Rubio. Photograph courtesy of Xavier L. Pellicer.

The Virgin Mary with Jesus Christ is the first of the series of Icons created in the St. Photios Shrine by two brothers, natives of Greece. The fresco paintings of George and John Filippakis will decorate the ceilings and walls of the shrine, depicting the spiritual dream of Greeks in America. Photograph by Randy Hoff.

During the Civil War, Government House served as the Provost Guard House for Federal troops. Photograph from the National Archives.

Government House, from a 1764 sketch preserved in the British Archives. The building was erected in 1706 to replace a two-story masonry house destroyed by siege in 1702. Renovation in 1759 gave it the appearance as drawn. The earliest known structure on the site was the house of Governor Gonzalo Canzo, built in 1604, later the official governor's residence and nucleus of legal and social activities. British Governor James Grant followed this tradition, occupying the house and modifying it to suit his needs. When Florida was returned to Spain, the building was again remodeled; old wood was replaced, walls were strengthened. Although some repairs were necessary in 1821, the United States found it adequate for use as a courthouse and civil building for newly arriving officials. It housed the first legislative council in 1823, maintaining the traditional role as center of legal administration. By 1833 it was necessary to rebuild the old residence. Federal funds were provided for the project and Robert Mills was commissioned as architect. The resulting sixteen-room structure housed the post office, federal offices, and courtroom. The name "Government House" was temporarily replaced by "The Courthouse." Drawing from the Historic St. Augustine Preservation Board.

Top:
After the Civil War, Government House, left, again functioned as a federal office building. Extensive remodeling in 1873 brought it to this stage, photographed in 1907. For sixty years the expanding post office department required increasingly more space, sharing the facilities primarily with the customs office. By the 1930s another renovation was necessary to accommodate the growth of the post office, customs office, and other federal agencies. Photograph courtesy of Mr. and Mrs. Robert W. Harper III.

Above:
In 1939 the enlarged facilities of Government House proudly maintained their civil functions. This arrangement was adequate for almost thirty years. In 1966 the building was transferred from the General Services Administration to the state of Florida as a public monument. Government House now serves as a museum, theater, and office area for the Historic St. Augustine Preservation Board, which administers it. Photograph from the Historic St. Augustine Preservation Board.

Chapter Three

The Second Spanish Regime: 1784-1821

The return of the Spanish brought about an era of social unrest and adjustment. Trade enterprises which had been developing over the years declined as the community juggled with economic and social changes wrought by the changing government. The official transfer of power came in July 1784, when Governor Vincente Manuel de Zéspedes accepted the province of East Florida for Spain. A few natives of the first Spanish regime returned to claim their former homes, but for several years many residences stood vacant and neglected.

The city typically relied on outside sources for subsistence, but a growing economy developed nevertheless. Jesse Fish continued to export oranges from his island grove. New plantations southwest of the city and west of the San Sebastian River flourished, replacing the formerly productive plantation of Lieutenant Governor Moultrie which now lay fallow, burned by wandering Indians. Although the indigo industry failed, the St. Johns River plantation of Francis Philip Fatio, Sr., continued to flourish through exportation of timber and other goods. John Leslie, the industrious trader who opened his firm of Panton, Leslie and Company, soon monopolized trade with the increasing number of Indians. His business proved a boon to St. Augustine since he often supplied the needs of the town when provisions were otherwise unavailable.

With the return of the Spanish came a revival of the Catholic faith. Since 1777 the Minorcan priest, Father Camps, had ministered to the Minorcans in the makeshift chapel of a St. George Street residence. Two Irish priests, Father Thomas Hassett and Father Michael O'Reilly, had been assigned to Florida as early as 1778 to replace the aging Father Camps and his assistant, Father Casanovas, who had departed before the New Smyrna emigrants marched to St. Augustine. Detained by the Revolutionary War, the prelates arrived in 1784, shortly after the new governor assumed office. By 1787 Father Hassett had opened a free school for the Minorcan children, and O'Reilly was busily calculating the parish

The Colonial Dames recently opened for the public the newly restored Ximene-Fatio House. The O'Reilly House and Don Toledo House balconies can be seen a short distance down Aviles Street in this 1979 view. Photograph by Randy Hoff.

needs of the outlying countryside. A significant contribution made during this period was the construction of the parish church, which was completed by 1797. Although gutted by fire in 1887, it was restored the following year and the Cathedral graces the plaza area today.

An attempt was made to build a Treasury; however, the walls of the unfinished structure only served as a reminder of the frustrations and discouragement experienced by the Spaniards as they struggled to develop the harbor town. The walls have long since fallen, but one memorial does remain—the coquina monument on the west end of the plaza, dedicated in 1812 to the liberal, though short-lived, constitution the *Cortez* offered to Spain.

The War of 1812 brought new problems to the Spanish city. The United States recognized the threat of invasion from across the Florida borders should the English acquire access to the Spanish territory. The animosity of the Florida Indians likewise spelled danger, and it appeared prudent to obtain the Spanish-held land, or at least defend the border against hostile activities. President Madison appointed two agents to negotiate with Spanish officials and, in the event of failure, seize the land when necessary. Revolutionary War general, Matthews, sent as agent to East Florida, conceived a plan by which farmers along the northern border would create an independent republic, later turning it over to the United States government. Fernandina patriots actually marched on St. Augustine, captured Fort Mosa (two miles north of the city), and demanded surrender of the town. The "patriots" and United States regulars camped north of town for several months, cutting off supplies from the countryside. After protests from Spanish and English officials, President Madison was forced to recall the regulars and reprimand his agents.

Friction between the United States and Spain continued after the conclusion of the War of 1812. Outlaw bands lived in the uncontrolled wilderness of interior Florida. English smugglers and renegades occupied Fernandina and Amelia Island,

This structure on the corner of Bridge and Marine streets is known as the Jose Simeon Sanchez House. It was built by George Long, Jr., who purchased the lot and a wooden house from Francisca Rosy Dulcet in 1804. The wooden house, built by Francisca's father, Jose Rosy, existed from 1788; the coquina structure was erected before 1821. Purchased by Jose Simeon Sanchez in 1835, it remained in his family until the 1930s. Beulah and William Aquilla Lewis purchased the house in the late 1930s, carefully restoring it during thirty years of occupancy. The historic house is now owned by Richard J. and Doris M. Quinn, brother and sister, who acquired the structure in 1975. Photograph from the St. Augustine Historical Society.

often encouraging the Seminoles to rebel against United States expansion. Runaway slaves sought refuge on Spanish-owned land. The situation was becoming intolerable for the Americans.

Finally, provoked by warring Georgia Seminoles, General Andrew Jackson entered the provinces, killing and capturing the Indians and their Negro allies and burning Indian and Spanish towns in his path. The Indians were subdued, but the prelude to the Seminole War of 1835-42 forced renegotiations for purchase of the southern land. In February 1819 a treaty was drafted, ceding the land to the United States government. All that remained was ratification by the two nations involved, a process which took two long years.

Antonio Proctor

A little-known figure in St. Augustine history is Antonio Proctor. Tony, as he was commonly called, was born a slave in 1743 on Jamaica. He arrived in the United States during the Revolutionary War as a body servant for a British officer and is said to have witnessed the Boston Tea Party. He apparently reached St. Augustine through the firm of Panton, Leslie and Company, who purchased him for use as an Indian interpreter. Although circumstances of his release from bondage are unknown, an 1816 Spanish document describes him as a *moreno libre* or "free man of lightly colored skin." The document, signed by Governor José Coppinger, granted Antonio Proctor 185 acres of land for "services faithfully renered." The land was situated about five miles west of St. Augustine and was a reward for his attempts to "pacify the province" during the War of 1812.

Proctor's close association with local Indians prompted historian Lee Warner to conclude that it was Proctor who enticed the Indians to aid the Spanish against the threat of American intrusion. Nevertheless, he proved his allegiance to the United States after the change of flags in 1821. Again serving as Indian interpreter, Tony worked closely with Governor William P. Duval and Indian Agent Gad Humphreys. Proctor received praise from Governor Duval for his truth and integrity.

In the 1830s, Proctor's association with St. Augustine diminished as he became involved with the development of the new town of Tallahassee. The lure of the capital city possibly evolved from his friendship with Doctor William H. Simmons, one of Tallahassee's founders.

Antonio Proctor left numerous descendants in Florida; several have distinguished themselves. Antonio's son, George, was an independent building contractor who constructed some of Tallahassee's finest antebellum houses. Two grandchildren represented their counties in the legislature during the Reconstruction period: John Proctor, from Leon County, served in the House of Representatives from 1873 to 1875 and again in 1879; he was a state senator in 1883 and 1885. George W. Proctor represented Jefferson County in the House in 1883.

Antonio Proctor died in Tallahassee in 1855, age 112, and was eulogized in a full column obituary printed in the *Florida Sentinel*.

Above:

The Benet family gather in the yard of their home on St. George and Cuna streets. Estevan Benet purchased the corner lot and a residence in 1804, later replacing the wooden building with a coquina structure. Estevan was the first Benet (Baineto or Beneto) to migrate to Florida from Minorca. He and Catalina Hernandez Benet parented four children. The eldest, Pedro (1798-1870), distinguished himself in St. Augustine: known as unofficial "king" of the Minorcans, his list of accomplishments included police officer, St. Johns County justice of the peace, church warden, alderman, mayor, and county commissioner. He was a director of the St. Johns and St. Augustine Canal Company and member of the Florida Historical Society from its organization in 1856. Pedro and one son, Joseph Ravina, operated a store located on the southwest corner of St. George and Cuna streets, a business maintained until the 1880s. It, and the Benet House, have been restored to their second Spanish period appearance. Photograph from the Historic St. Augustine Preservation Board.

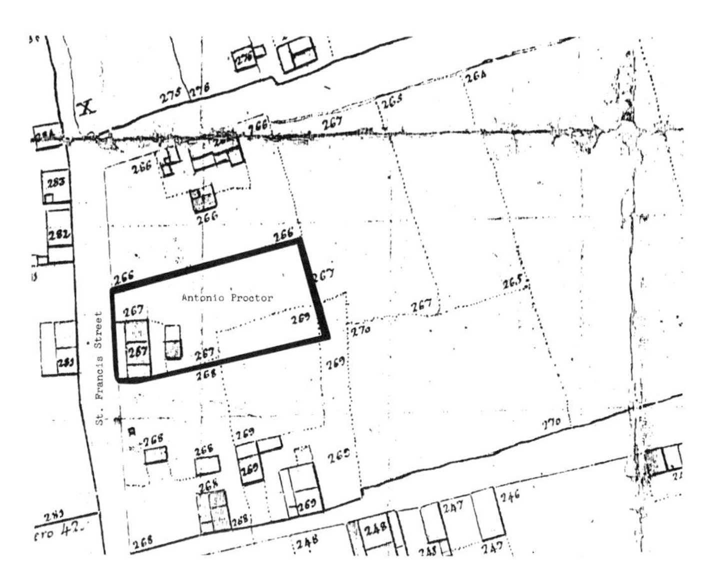

Antonio Proctor's St. Francis Street house (as it appears on the Rocque map) consisted of a three-room structure with a two-room detached kitchen. The substantial lot, which measured approximately 66 feet by 144 feet, was purchased in 1820 and sold in 1830. Proctor disposed of the 185 acres of land given him by Governor Coppinger in 1824, before migrating to Tallahassee. Map from the Historic St. Augustine Preservation Board.

Two St. Augustine descendants of Antonio Proctor are John Proctor and his great-grandnephew, Phillip Twine, shown here in 1964. They stand beside Dawson Chapel, the Christian-Methodist-Episcopal Church which the Proctor family was instrumental in establishing in 1909. Photograph courtesy of Henry Twine.

This photograph, looking south on Aviles Street, shows the stately Ximenez-Fatio house with the wing extension visible in the rear. When Spaniard Andres Ximenez built it around 1798, the two-story coquina and masonry structure included a store within the main house, an adjoining warehouse (the west wing in the photo) and a detached kitchen—still extant but obscured by foliage in this picture. Major remodeling was undertaken between 1830-48, at which time the warehouse roofs were removed and a wood frame second story and balcony were added. A wooden floor covered the original masonry floors and, in general, accommodations for boarders were expanded and improved. The structure functioned as an inn for much of its existence and can be toured in that mode today. Photograph courtesy of Dorothy Dunham Olson.

Boarders dutifully pose outside the Ximenez-Fatio House on Hospital (Aviles) Street in this pre-Civil War photograph. It is possible that the figure in the first floor window is Louisa Fatio, the last of a succession of women associated with the operation of the residence and boarding house. First was Juana Ximenez, wife of the original owner, Andres Ximenez. Juana, the daughter of Minorcan leader Francisco Pellicer, assisted her husband in business and helped operate the store contained within the house. Neither Juana nor her husband lived long after construction of the house was completed. Margaret Cook became the second owner in 1830, apparently remodeling the structure extensively to accommodate boarders. She enlisted the aid of Elizabeth C. Whitehurst, a friend and widow who operated the inn until Margaret Cook sold it in 1938. The purchaser was Sarah Petty Anderson, a widow who chose this genteel occupation as a means of supporting herself and her family. The reputation of the boarding house was well known by the time Louise Fatio purchased the house in 1855, and she maintained the high standards of the establishment throughout her years of management. At her death in 1875 at age 79, the property passed into the hands of the Dunham family through Louisa Fatio's nephew, Fatio Dunham. Judge David Dunham sold the house to the Florida branch of the Colonial Dames of America in 1939. The members of that organization have recently restored the house to its 1830-48 appearance, stressing its unique position throughout the nineteenth century as haven to some of Florida's earliest tourists. Photograph from the St. Augustine Historical Society.

Long considered the oldest surviving frame structure in St. Augustine, this early nineteenth century building on St. George Street has inspired legends and stimulated memories for decades. Juan Gianopoly, a New Smyrna emigrant and a carpenter by trade, constructed the original frame dwelling on this lot shortly after purchasing the property in 1778. Although the present structure varies in size and shape from the original, the British-Colonial appearance reflects the probable style of the earlier home, which was undoubtably influenced during the English occupation. Gianopoly later became a successful dairy farmer and bequeathed his property to his heirs after his death in the 1820s. The house with its detached kitchen has offered services in numerous forms. Its location near the City Gate was ideal for photographers, as shown in this 1920s photograph, or as a tea room and gift shop, as Hanna Erwin discovered around 1918. It now represents the oldest schoolhouse, a function it may have had in the nineteenth century when schoolmasters taught small classes in the first floor room with the last "graduates" attending in 1864. Photograph by H.M. Tucker; courtesy of Howard Hanson.

Noel Wallace Mier (1879-1935) was the great-grandson of a second Spanish period resident, Antonio Fernandez de Mier, born in Cadiz, Spain, in 1777. Antonio arrived in St. Augustine sometime before March 1814 and married Ana Margarita de Ortego, of Minorcan descent. Mier was vice-president of the Florida East Coast Railway. Photograph courtesy of Mr. and Mrs. Russell Mier.

Far right:
Clara Butler Lopez Mier (1879-1963) sits with her catch after a successful day on the bay in the 1930s. Behind her is Ketterlinus Junior High School. She was elected St. Augustine's Woman of the Year in 1960. In addition to her numerous charitable works Clara Mier was known as a successful restaurateur; her several establishments included Clara's El Patio on Aviles and Charlotte streets. Photograph courtesy of Mr. and Mrs. Russell Mier.

Right:
Inez Noda Colee sits with her children Isabella, right, Loretta, and young Charles, standing behind his mother. The Noda family originated on the isle of Gomera in the Canaries and appeared in St. Augustine in 1804; they were rapidly assimilated into the predominantly Minorcan community. Jose de Noda married Aqueda Villalonga in St. Augustine in 1805, and of their offspring, three married descendants of New Smyrna colonists. Rosa married Celestino Leonardi, Thomasa married John C. Canova, and Antonio married Antonia Rogero. Photograph courtesy of Charles Colee.

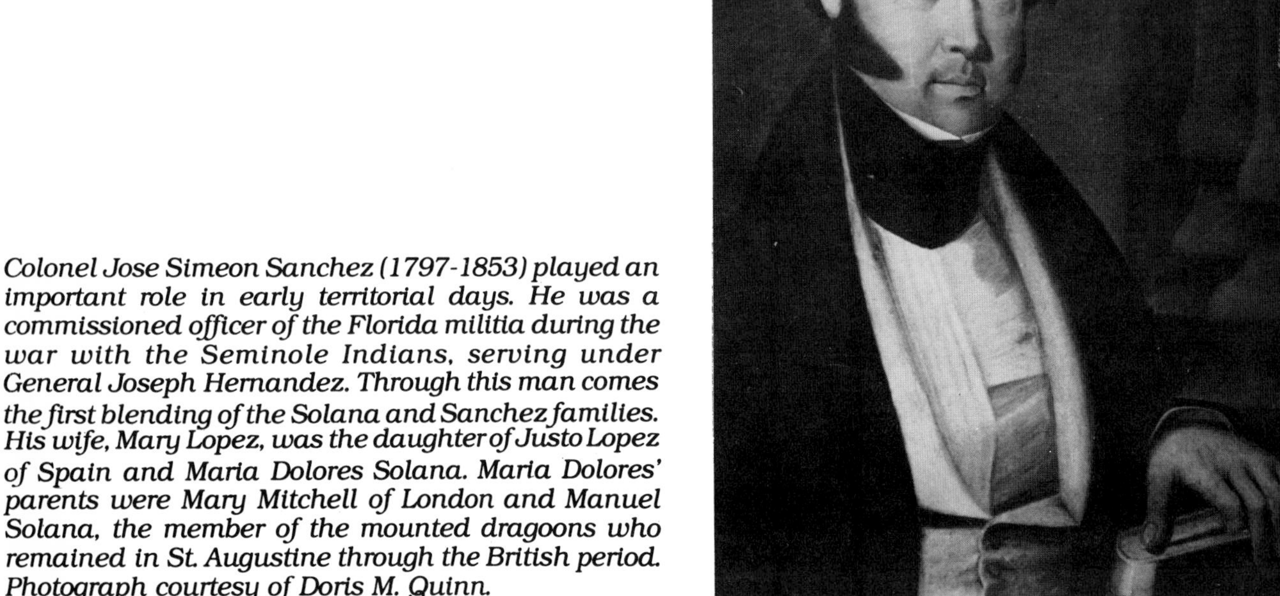

Colonel Jose Simeon Sanchez (1797-1853) played an important role in early territorial days. He was a commissioned officer of the Florida militia during the war with the Seminole Indians, serving under General Joseph Hernandez. Through this man comes the first blending of the Solana and Sanchez families. His wife, Mary Lopez, was the daughter of Justo Lopez of Spain and Maria Dolores Solana. Maria Dolores' parents were Mary Mitchell of London and Manuel Solana, the member of the mounted dragoons who remained in St. Augustine through the British period. Photograph courtesy of Doris M. Quinn.

Jesse Fish's residence on Anastasia Island was sketched in 1867 by Henry J. Morton. Fish, a British subject, was sent to St. Augustine in 1736 at about ten years of age. He lived with a prominent Spanish family, learning local customs and language to represent a British firm in New York. The firm, Walton's Company, supplied provisions to the Spanish garrison, and Fish became their liaison with the foreign community. Apparently he learned the language and his duties well. He spanned three eras of early St. Augustine's history, remaining when the British took occupancy and again when the Spanish returned. He was instrumental in executing property exchanges for evacuees, often to his own advantage since houses and land were left unprotected. His beautiful estate, El Vergel, ("garden") on the Island, became internationally known for the oranges Fish grew and exported from his forty-acre orchard. Jesse Fish died in 1790, leaving behind much mystery and intrigue about his life and dealings within the community. Drawing from the St. Augustine Historical Society.

The Worth House, a second Spanish period residence erected in 1791, received its name decades later from occupants Margaret S. Worth (widow of Seminole and Mexican War General William J. Worth) and her daughter of the same name. The Worth women owned the structure from 1868 to 1905. Previous owners William Livingston and daughter, Hester, resided in the Marine Street house from 1817 to 1869, converting it into the Union Hotel from 1819 to 1830. The historic structure was razed in 1960 and a reconstruction using the original coquina walls was built on a lot bounded by Marine Street and Avenida Menendez. Photograph from the Florida Photographic Archives, Strozier Library, F. S. U.

MAP OF
FLORIDA
G E O R G I A
GULF OF
MEXICO
APPALACHIE BAY
MOSQUITO
MONROE
A L A B A M A
GULF OF MEXICO
WEST PART
FLORIDA

Chapter Four

Territorial Days and Early Statehood: 1821-1888

St. Johns County, the dark area in the northeast portion of the state, was one of twelve counties delineated on this 1823 map. With the dawn of the territorial era, the new governor of the Provinces of Florida, Major General Andrew Jackson, declared "all country east of the river Suwaney [sic] should be designated county of St. Johns." The ordinance, signed at Pensacola in 1821, ostensibly created a county encompassing half the state. The following year Dural was added to St. Johns, and Jackson County was included within Escambia. By 1823 the county had diminished considerably. As the state developed, more counties were created from the older, larger territories, and St. Johns County continued to shrink. The last county formed within its boundaries was Flagler, established in 1917. Map from the St. Augustine Historical Society.

The Spanish colors floated silently down the tall flagpole on the Castillo grounds on July 10, 1821, officially ending an extraordinary epoch in the life of the 256-year-old city. Spanish sovereignty had been interrupted only by the twenty-year span of British rule. Now the last Spanish governor, José Coppinger, transferred possession of the province of East Florida to Colonel Robert Butler, representative of Governor Andrew Jackson. Florida was at last a territory of the United States of America.

Speculators and fortune-hunters flocked to the novel old city on the heels of United States offilcials. The Minorcan element, including the Greek and Italian descendants of Turnbull's colony, watched as newcomers flooded the town. A few Spanish residents also remained, resulting in an admixture of dialects and languages echoing in the narrow streets of the foreign-flavored city.

Coping with the influx of immigrants was a problem overshadowed by the sudden appearance of yellow fever in the city. By the fall the disease had reached epidemic proportions, forcing many new arrivals to depart as quickly as they had come. A new cemetery, the Huguenot or Protestant Cemetery, became the burial ground for numerous non-Catholic victims of the disease.

Beset by problems, the new administration under Governor Jackson continued to advance nonetheless. A town council was formed under the direction of Secretary William Worthington, the official responsible for establishing civilian government in the eastern portion of the state, now declared St. Johns County. United States soldiers were quartered in St. Francis Barracks, and the Castillo was renamed Fort Marion in honor of Revolutionary War General Francis Marion. The metamorphosis was gradual, but undeniable.

The early years of territorial growth perhaps marked the genesis of Florida's great tourist industry. Two renowned visitors in the 1820s were Ralph Waldo Emerson, who came to improve his health, and Prince Napoleon Achille Murat, the son of the king of Naples and nephew of Napoleon

Union soldiers contemplate the pyramids commemorating Major Francis L. Dade and the 110 soldiers massacred by rebel Indians. Photograph from the St. Augustine Historical Society.

Bonaparte. Murat became a familiar figure in St. Augustine, reputedly residing for a time in a small house on south St. George Street.

A deterrent to prospective visitors was the Seminole Indian conflict which threatened the safety of settlers and travelers alike. Since the early 1800s the United States had attempted to subdue the rebellious faction, despite the strenuous objections of Spanish officials. The new American governor was no friend to the Indian and lost no time in arranging a "home" for the Seminoles in central Florida.

As white settlers moved into Florida territory, inconsistent demands were made upon the Indians and their Negro allies. They were forced by law to remain on the reservation, yet denounced for impeding the progress of settlers wishing to develop the mid-section of the territory.

The decision to remove all Seminoles from Florida sparked the wrath of the warrior Osceola, whose anger exploded throughout the white communities. Spurred to action by the Seminole leader, a warrior called Alligator massacred almost all of the 110 soldiers sent to reinforce Fort King (present site of Ocala). Three pyramidal monuments in the National Cemetery on St. Augustine's Marine street cover the remains of the murdered men and their commanding officer, Major Francis L. Dade. On that same December day in 1835, Osceola took the lives of at least seven men. One of those killed, a general, had previously imprisoned the rebel Indian for voicing objections to the removal project.

For eight years the bloody battles raged, until the Seminoles were either transported to the west or forced into seclusion in the swamps of south Florida. Osceola, captured under a flag of truce near the present St. Johns County community of Moultrie, died in January 1839 from illness contracted while incarcerated in South Carolina. Although the threat of Seminole uprising recurred in the 1850s (resulting in further western emigration), the close of the Second Seminole War in 1842 marked the beginning of a period of peace for the countryside.

Wartime restrictions did not altogether inhibit activity in the old city. The presence of the military had enriched it economically and enlivened the somewhat dreary town. The wooden walls of the Florida House hotel arose in 1835 to accommodate the overflow of soldiers and refugees from out of town. The year 1838 brought the completion of an extensive seawall and the opening of a new store operated by Burroughs E. Carr. The freeze of 1835 had destroyed the orange trees, but Dr. Andrew Anderson quickly replaced the money crop with a new one—mulberry trees for the silk industry. Dr. Seth Peck arrived in the city in 1832, soon assuming the practice of retiring Dr. Anderson. St. Augustine was guided through the difficult decade of the 1830s by responsible citizens such as Doctors Peck and Anderson, Judge Joseph Lee Smith, Benjamin A. Putnam, and Burroughs E. Carr.

Tallahassee, the territorial capital since 1824, had already robbed St. Augustine of its legislative status, but visitors were still drawn to the quaint old city with the balmy, salubrious breezes. Boarding houses filled to capacity during the winter months, and the increasing need for accommodations produced the finest hotel St. Augustine had boasted to date, the Magnolia. Its days of glory were numbered, however, for the Civil War abruptly ended the tourist trade, leaving occupied St. Augustine reliant on its blue-coated wardens to provide a semblance of income as it limped through the 1860s.

As was the case with so many Southern cities, St. Augustine survived the war, scarred and exhausted, but eager to regain its former vitality. The St. Johns Railway from Tocoi, bought by William Astor in 1870, was rebuilt and improved. Travel resumed, and greater quantities of visitors flocked to the ancient city. The smell of orange blossoms drifted from the prosperous groves that replaced the trees destroyed in 1835. The dream of public schooling was realized both in the county and in the city. Unwittingly, St. Augustine prepared for the golden years of the future.

José Mariano Hernandez (1788-1856) was born in St. Augustine of Minorcan parents. Educated in Havana and Savannah, he became a prestigious figure in the second Spanish and territorial periods. During the Spanish regime, he served as interpreter and practiced law. After the change of flags in 1821, President Monroe appointed Hernandez one of twelve members of the legislative council. He achieved the rank of brigadier general in the Florida Volunteers during the Second Seminole War, and acting under orders from Major General Thomas S. Jesup, captured the Indian leader, Osceola. Photograph from the St. Augustine Historical Society.

Trinity Episcopal Church

The formal history of Trinity Episcopal Parish began when the Stars and Stripes first flew above St. Augustine in 1821. However, the first Protestant services in Florida date from the beginning of the British period (1763). Services were conducted in the English Constitution House, a structure occupying the present site of Trinity Church. Under the direction of the Reverend John Forbes, a house of worship was erected on south St. George Street, now the location of St. Joseph Academy tennis courts. Architectural sketches indicate the edifice boasted a large tower and steeple. Dedicated in 1773 as St. Peter's, the structure fell into disrepair during the second Spanish occupancy and was eventually razed. St. Peter's Chapel in the present church kindles the memory of this first Protestant sanctuary.

When Florida became a United States possession, plans were instituted for the creation of an Episcopal parish. The Reverend Andrew Fowler was sent to St. Augustine to organize a church, and Trinity's cornerstone was laid in 1825.

It is interesting to note the familiar names on the early rolls. Edmund Kirby-Smith (destined to become a Confederate general) was the first infant baptized in the church. Reuben Loring, father of General William Wing Loring, did masonry work and plastered the walls. Abraham DuPont was a prominent member, as was George Gibbs III, the first warden. Early 1900s records give testimony to the dedication of well-known families such as the Edward S. Vaills, the Reginald Whites and the David L. Dunhams.

Major reconstruction occurred at the turn of the century. With the exception of the north transept and the baptistry, the church was completely rebuilt. Now a cruciform structure capable of seating 500, Florida's oldest Protestant church is a lasting memorial to St. Augustine's past.

Episcopalians worshiped in this building from 1825 until major remodeling occurred at the turn of the century. Photograph courtesy of Trinity Parish Episcopal Church.

The spire of cypress shingles remains unchanged since the construction of the original Trinity Church. It remains a landmark today as it was in this 1919 view. Photograph courtesy of Trinity Parish Episcopal Church.

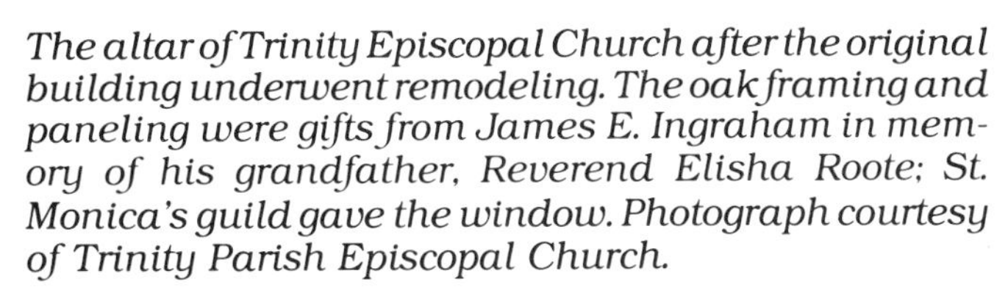

The altar of Trinity Episcopal Church after the original building underwent remodeling. The oak framing and paneling were gifts from James E. Ingraham in memory of his grandfather, Reverend Elisha Roote; St. Monica's guild gave the window. Photograph courtesy of Trinity Parish Episcopal Church.

St. Peter's Chapel commemorates the original Trinity Parish Church as well as the first Anglican church for which it is named. The north and east walls are part of the original structure erected in 1825; the altar and altar rail were part of the first sanctuary. The impressive Tiffany window adds interest with the illusion of the disappearing angel: the angel on the left is clearly distinguishable at half-light, but fades from view under bright or dim illumination. The baptismal font, (left), is dedicated to the Reverend Francis Rutledge, who was elected first bishop of the diocese of Florida in 1851. Reverend Rutledge led Trinity's congregation from 1840 to 1845. Photograph by Jim Donovan; courtesy of Trinity Parish Episcopal Church.

George Rainsford Fairbanks (1820-1906) arrived in St. Augustine in 1842 to fill the newly vacated position of clerk of superior court. Throughout his years as resident of the city he became politically involved, serving as state senator in 1846-47 and mayor of the city in 1857. However, it is his remarkable contribution to the history of Florida and St. Augustine that bears mention. His early interest in the development of Florida prompted mastery of the Spanish language in order to read the ancient documents in their original form. Perhaps also inspired by historian Buckingham Smith, Fairbanks undertook to establish an organization promoting historical studies of the city and state. Toward this end, Fairbanks assembled a group of illustrious gentlemen in 1855 and planted the seed of interest. By 1856 the Florida Historical Society was formally organized with officers including Major Benjamin A. Putnam, George Burt, K. B. Gibbs, and Fairbanks, who served as one of five vice-presidents. The following year showed a membership of 134. It was then that Fairbanks read his lengthy essay "The Early History of Florida," the forerunner of the scholarly publication The History and Antiquities of the City of St. Augustine. *The volume, published in 1858, was the first serious historical account of the city and the first study utilizing Spanish records and documents. Photograph from the Florida Historical Society.*

Thomas Buckingham Smith (1810-71), diplomat, scholar, and humanitarian, left an unprecedented legacy to Floridians, particularly residents of the nation's oldest city. Through his efforts as amateur historian, Smith compiled a prodigious collection of documentary materials of Florida's creation. Smith displayed an early interest in Florida's Spanish history, perhaps prompted by a visit to Mexico at age fourteen while his father served as United States consul. Later, while practicing law in St. Augustine, Smith's interest in historical research expanded, compelling him to seek appointment as secretary to the United States legation at Mexico City. There he spent his days copying ancient manuscripts in the Spanish archives, later publishing historical articles about the priceless documents. The procedure was repeated from 1855 to 1858 while Smith served in Madrid, Spain. By 1860 Smith returned to St. Augustine, possessor of invaluable books and transcripts, and renewed an acquaintance with historian George Fairbanks, whose own work was influenced by Smith's discoveries. Photograph from the Florida Historical Society.

Civil War Years

The mood in the city was jubilant in January 1861, when Major Benjamin A. Putnam announced Florida's decision to secede from the Union. Within days a Fernandina contingent of the Florida Volunteers slipped past a Federal revenue cutter and entered St. Augustine's harbor with orders to seize the Federal military installation, Fort Marion. The mission was easily accomplished, with St. Augustine Blues assisting in the "capture." Although St. Augustine feared eventual reprisals, inhabitants of the ancient city initially felt the pinch of war in their pocketbooks and growling stomachs as blockades prevented the flow of supplies into the town. But by March 1862 it was painfully apparent that Federal troops were at the doorstep. On the eleventh day of that month, Commander C. R. P. Rogers came ashore with a small landing party to be met by acting mayor Christobal Bravo. Mayor Bravo escorted the officers and men to Government House, where the city council quickly and quietly acknowledged the authority of the United States. The town soon settled into peaceful coexistence with the uniformed captors, gratefully experiencing an economic resurgence with the influx of money and food.

Although a Southern city, St. Augustine always maintained strong Northern ties, and from the outset of the conflict Union sympathies were openly espoused by the Anderson family, Buckingham Smith, George Burt, and schoolmistress Sarah Mathers. Friendships were strained, particularly among those whose husbands and sons fought in the uniform of the Confederacy. Frances Smith, mother of Confederate General Edmund Kirby-Smith, maintained a cool but cordial relationship with Clarissa Anderson, at the same time refusing to cooperate with the Federal authorities. Divided sympathies created an atmosphere of bitterness and anger. A shooting incident finally provoked action, forcing Colonel H. S. Putnam to demand a signed oath of allegiance to

This Civil War period scene shows the Tovar House, (right background), on St. Francis and Charlotte streets. It was photographed by Union soldier Sam Cooley. Photograph from the National Archives.

In 1864 Federal troops stand outside the Provost Marshal's Office building on King and Hospital (Aviles) streets, once the residence of S. M. Wakeman. Photograph from the National Archives.

Union soldiers occupied this house on the bayfront during the Civil War. The building, called the Cobb House on an 1855 city sketch, was probably the winter residence of New Yorker, Nathan Cobb. North of the structure stands the store and the home of Burroughs E. Carr, with the familiar coquina arch in between. 1864 photograph from the National Archives.

Union soldiers occupied Fort Marion during the Civil War. Photograph from the Library of Congress.

the United States from all males over the age of fourteen. The threat of expulsion from town loomed as a consequence of refusal. Over a period of months, hundreds of residents, primarily women and children, were displaced from their city. Frances Smith and her sister Helen, wife of lawyer Benjamin Putnam, were among the last forced to depart from their hometown.

Perhaps St. Augustine fared better than most Southern towns; no troops stormed the city and no battles raged in nearby fields. Yet the gloom of war clouds darkened the homes and hearts of St. Augustine residents as they watched the city slowly decay. By the time news of Lee's surrender was announced (one month late), the populace could only breathe a sigh of relief. Houses had fallen into disrepair and the bridge over the San Sebastian River had been destroyed.

Families grieved for the young men who would never return. However, there was pride in the city for the sons who had fought bravely for the South, particularly three men who achieved high ranks in the army of the Confederacy. Colonel George Couper Gibbs was a native son who was welcomed home after an agonizing summer as a defendant and witness in the Andersonville war crimes trial. General Edmund Kirby-Smith settled in Tennessee after the war, teaching mathematics at the University of the South.

General William Wing Loring is memorialized in the city by a monument west of Government House. A resident of St. Augustine from age five, Loring discovered the military at an early age, fighting for the Florida militia in the 1830s and later distinguishing himself in the United States Army during the War with Mexico in the mid-1840s. After the Civil War, Loring chose to continue soldiering, joining a military staff of Civil War veterans formed by the Khedive in Egypt.

With the war years over, the crumbling community slowly picked up the pieces. As it regained strength and vitality, it drew ever closer to the era of greatest prosperity—the days of luxury hotels, lavish entertainment, and Henry Morrison Flagler.

Edmund Kirby-Smith (1824-93) was a St. Augustine native whose distinguished military career included duty in the Mexican War, a teaching tour at West Point, and service in Texas. In 1861 he entered the Confederate service, rapidly rising to the rank of brigadier general. He was one of the last Confederate generals in the field when he surrendered to General Canby in May 1865. At the time of his death in 1893, General Kirby-Smith was the sole surviving full general of the Confederacy. Photograph from the St. Augustine Historical Society.

This Aviles Street building was the birthplace of Edmund Kirby-Smith. The 1902 photo shows a garden view of the structure in its function as public library. Photograph from the Florida Photographic Archives, Strozier Library, F. S. U.

The street side of the Kirby-Smith residence in 1979. The public library still occupies the building, although plans are in effect for a move to new quarters. In the early 1880s the Daily Press, *a forerunner of the present* St. Augustine Record, *operated in the building. The newspaper eventually became the* Weekly Record *and then the* St. Augustine Evening Record, *publishing from the same place. The* St. Augustine Record *now operates from its Cordova Street location. Photograph by Randy Hoff.*

Colonel George Couper Gibbs (1822-73) was the youngest of six children of George Gibbs III and Isabella Kingsley. He was born the year after the family emigrated from North Carolina to Florida. He achieved the rank of colonel in the Confederate Army. Photograph courtesy of Margaret Gibbs Watt.

This Civil War-period structure was the residence of Colonel George Couper Gibbs. The site is presently occupied by the St. Augustine Art Association building. Photograph courtest of Margaret Gibbs Watt.

An 1887 view of St. George Street between Treasury and Cathedral streets. The building on the left was occupied at one time by the Sisters of Mercy, who were petitioned by Bishop Verot in 1857 to teach in the city. Photograph from the Historic St. Augustine Preservation Board.

Left:
Jean-Pierre Augustin Marcellin Verot (1829-76), the first bishop of St. Augustine, is portrayed here by local artist Jean Wagner Troemel. Father Verot departed his homeland, France, in 1830 to teach in Baltimore, Maryland. Twenty-two years later he was assigned a pastorate in nearby Ellicott City and was serving in that capacity when, in 1858, he learned of his unexpected appointment to the new vicariate of Florida. Following his consecration as bishop, he embarked southward, reaching St. Augustine in June. In 1859, realizing the need for greater ministry in the "holy poor" vicariate, Verot obtained seven priests from France for pastoral duty throughout the state. Later that year he petitioned five Sisters of Mercy from Connecticut to open the first convent school; three Christian Brothers came from Canada to begin a boys' day school. The Civil War impeded progress, but did not quench the spirit of the "Rebel Bishop" who staunchly defended Southern rights. With the return of peace, the Sisters of Mercy reopened St. Mary's Academy, and Verot traveled to his birthplace of Le Puy to beg assistance from the Sisters of St. Joseph. He chose eight nuns from the sixty enthusiastic volunteers. With unflagging energy, the prelate rebuilt the war-torn vicariate, restoring it to far greater strength by the end of the decade. His concern for the freed black slaves was evidenced in his efforts to improve circumstances and increase educational opportunities for the freedmen.

From 1861 to 1870, Verot administered his Florida duties from Savannah, Georgia, having been called there as third bishop of the diocese. When the new diocese of St. Augustine was created in 1870, Verot requested a transfer and returned to the city as its first bishop. Bishop Verot died in St. Augustine following one of his frequent trips about the state. He lies in the mortuary chapel vault in Tolomato Cemetery. Portrait courtesy of Jean Wagner Troemel.

The O'Reilly House, right, on Aviles Street was the rectory of Don Miguel O'Reilly, Chaplain of Troops and pastor of the Catholic Parish. Father O'Reilly arrived in St. Augustine in 1784, occupying the rectory until his death in 1812. In his will he stated that the house should be used for future religious women educators. The stipulation was met in 1867 when the Sisters of St. Joseph moved to the house, at the same time opening a school for black children in a nearby stone building. After successive use as a convent, school, residence for retired persons, and later a storage area, the house was restored and opened to the public as a heritage home. Photograph from the Historic St. Augustine Preservation Board.

In 1879 the Sisters of St. Joseph moved from the O'Reilly house to a new three-story, coquina convent-school on St. George Street, thus making the founding of St. Joseph's Academy. This photo, circa, 1886, shows the entrance to the convent and academy and the coquina structure that was opened by the Sisters in 1867 as a free school for Negroes. In the early 1900s stone from the building was used to fashion a wall encircling a new academy complex. Photograph courtesy of the Historic St. Augustine Preservation Board.

This 1946 view shows St. Joseph's Academy after remodeling. Wooden porches were replaced by concrete additions, and new enclosures gave unity to the complex. The facades were redesigned to give architectural harmony, and the center gate was replaced. Two new entrances were formed, one leading to St. Joseph's Convent, right, and one to the academy buildings. The oldest Catholic high school in Florida has continued to grow and develop. Over one hundred graduating classes have received diplomas achieved through classwork in the historic halls. Insufficient space has necessitated relocation to new facilities currently being erected on property off State Road 207. Photograph courtesy of St. Joseph's Academy.

A young woman stands before the academy gate in 1910, shortly after major construction was completed. The gate opened into the center of the complex, leading to two new classroom buildings and the old coquina structure which became solely a convent. Photograph courtesy of St. Joseph's Academy.

The Fine Arts Building of St. Joseph's Academy was designed by architect Alexander Jackson Davis, whose work includes the North Carolina State Capitol and several buildings on the campus of the University of North Carolina at Chapel Hill. Built in 1875-76 as the winter residence of Robert D. and Isabel Donaldson Bronson, the early-colonial-style structure stands today with minimal deviation from architectural plans. The full porch is a modification of a smaller portico extending a few feet from either side of the entry and second-story window on the side. In 1966 the three-tiered fountain was moved to its present location in front of the Lightner Museum. Photograph courtesy of St. Joseph's Academy.

Right:
In 1797 the completed walls of the Cathedral graced the center of the city. The Spanish design and Moorish belfry added charm to the plaza area and, until the 1887 fire, the four bells chimed the Angelus three times a day. Only the walls remained after the structure was consumed by flames; however, restoration the following year included the addition of a new chancel and transepts as well as the stately campanile that rises above the city. Photograph from the Historic St. Augustine Preservation Board.

Villa Flora, located across from St. Joseph's Academy, serves as the house of formation (Novitiate) for the sisters. The building was constructed for Reverend and Mrs. O.A. Weenolsen in 1898, and was the winter residence of Bessie (Mrs. Alanson) Wood when this circa 1911 photograph was taken. The design of this splendid example of a Flagler era "winter cottage" was probably inspired by the Moorish Revival style of Villa Zorayda. The cottage served as a hotel, restaurant, gift shop, and kindergarten prior to ownership by the Sisters of St. Joseph. Photograph courtesy of B.M. Hall.

Coach Slade Pinkham led the St. Joseph's Academy Eagles to victory in six of seven tournaments played between 1932 and 1938. Left to right, bottom row: Le Verne Powers Alexander, Margaret Poli, Virginia (Jimmy) Poland Salvador, Ruthie Nordmann, Vivian Dineen, Norma Clarke Poli; second row: Catherine Sands, Jane Arthur, Alice Robinson, Anna De Grande, Rose Fazio; top row: Jeanette Flayfiel, Mary Triay Casto, Dorothy Rico, Rosita Walsh; standing: Father J. H. O'Keefe, director of athletics, and Coach Slade D. Pinkham; standing against flagpole: Assistant Coach Wade Noda, with Marion Powers, manager Anita Ortez, and Mercedes Colee, behind sign. Photograph courtesy of Slade D. Pinkham.

The Cathedral-Basilica

St. Augustine, the birthplace of Christianity in our nation, long deserved a Catholic house of worship worthy of its historic distinction. It was Father Thomas Hassett who obtained the site in 1793 and began construction of the holy place. Several years later Father Michael O'Reilly witnessed the realization of the dream, participating in the church's dedication in December 1797. The original building was a rectangular structure 120 feet long and 42 feet wide. The oldest of the four bells bears the date 1689 and may have come from the ruins of the old Nombre de Dios chapel. In 1870 the diocese of St. Augustine was formed and the church was designated a Cathedral.

The walls remaining after the 1887 fire now comprise the portion of the Cathedral south of the transept. A new transept and chancel were part of major restoration, which also included erection of the commanding bell tower. Additional renovation was accomplished by Archbishop Joseph B. Hurley in 1965, at which time the sanctuary was enlarged and the Chapel of the Blessed Sacrament built.

The magnificent interior of the Cathedral reflects a Spanish heritage embellished by ornate decor. The reredos behind the high altar is composed of the original marble framed with carved wood of white and gold colors accented with gold burnish. The suspended figure of Christ is also carved wood with similar white, pure gold, and gold burnish coloration. Murals throughout the Cathedral depict relevant historical and religious events; the life of the patron Saint Augustine is illustrated in twelve windows in the transepts and nave.

In December 1976 the Cathedral was elevated to the status of Basilica, an honor bestowed because of its historical significance.

A bayfront landmark from before the 1840s, this extant structure was reconstructed after the 1887 conflagration that gutted the Cathedral. It was rebuilt from poured concrete to its stately appearance as photographed here in 1902. Originally the residence of merchant and hotel owner Burroughs E. Carr, it was later occupied by another prominent businessman, Bartolo Genovar, resident from 1895 to 1912. Ownership following the Genovar family includes Mrs. G. G. MacLennon, Homer H. McKeehan, J. Roy Hellier, Aline G. Hellier, and W. I. Drysdale, who purchased the house in 1952. Now the Chart House restaurant, its spacious rooms provide a pleasant atmosphere for diners. Photograph from the Florida Photographic Archives, Strozier Library, F.S.U.

The Catholic rectory nestled beside the tall Cathedral campanile when a photographer captured this scene in 1902. The concrete structure was completed by the early 1880s; the gracefully sculptured stone wall replaced a picket fence sometime before the turn of the century. The bishop's house was razed in 1965, leaving a spacious courtyard now occupied by a statue commemorating the Minorcan priest, Father Pedro Camps. Photograph from the Florida Photographic Archives, Strozier Library, F. S. U.

Right:
The facade of the restored Cathedral closely resembles the original structure. The bells still hung silently at the time of this 1950s photograph, but were refurbished in the mid-sixties and now ring electrically from the four niches in the belfry. Preserved within the Cathedral archives are the oldest written records of American origin, documents uncovered by Bishop Verot after extensive searching in Havana. Brought to the United States by Bishop William J. Kenny, these records include documents dating from Solana-Visente marriage in 1594. Also contained within these walls is the "Golden Book of the Minorcans," the meticulously written records of Father Camps, priest of the New Smyrna colony. Photograph courtesy of St. Joseph's Academy.

GAS

The Roscoe Perry family are surrounded by orange trees on their Noda Concession property. Perry purchased the land in 1869, selling it fifteen years later to William Warden, who erected the large Moorish edifice now housing Ripley's Museum. Oak trees still gracing the property were planted by the Perry family. Left to right: Margaret, Charles, Helen, Mary S., William, Margarita (Mrs. Roscoe), and Roscoe Perry. Photograph courtesy of Eleanor Philips Barnes.

Abbott Tract

The Abbott Tract name refers to land extending from the north boundary of the Castillo reservation (formerly called Clinch Street) approximately to Pine Street, with San Marco and the bayfront forming west and east boundaries. It was purchased in territorial days by William G. Davis and Peter Sken Smith, becoming the first residential area developed outside colonial city limits. In 1838 Smith divided his property into thirty-two lots named the Noda Concession for the previous Spanish owner. The rapid sales and resulting construction also prompted Davis to subdivide his portion of land, a section running from Joiner to a short distance north of Pine Street. An influential developer of Noda Concession was John C. Cleland, who established North City Wharf, a steam sawmill, and the North City Hotel on the property.

Following the Civil War, the property was acquired by Lucy Abbott and William and Mary Van Ness. Six of the eight houses constructed by Lucy Abbott were erected between 1872 and 1885, and faced east on Water Street. By 1904 the number of residences had increased from a dozen to more than 120 and were occupied by physicians, bankers, a retired military general, and other prominent citizens. Many black employees of the homeowners built on adjoining Abbott Tract property, primarily on Pine and Osceola streets. The configuration of these smaller houses indicates that roads were nonexistent at the time of construction. About one-third of the population of Abbott Tract was comprised of blacks by the turn of the century.

Perry Place on Water Street was built in 1885 and is pictured here in 1900. The one-story addition, right, was rented by C. F. Hamblen as a grocery store before it was moved to its present location alongside the house for use as a kitchen. The house is now the residence of Mr. and Mrs. Dan Stoddard.

Roscoe Perry is on the roof. Others are, from left to right: Lillian Stevens, Anne Kemper, Margaret Kemper, Ernest Kemper, Helen Perry Smith (formerly Kemper, mother of Kemper and Smith children), baby Edward Smith, Frank Smith in wagon, Mary Perry Philips, Clarence R. Philips in front of his mother, Ann Stevens, Margarita Capo Perry. Photograph courtesy of Ellie Shepherd (Mrs. Roscoe) Pomar.

The elegant Queen Anne residence of bank president John T. Dismukes was built on north Water Street around 1890. The building, shown here around 1910, is the oldest surviving brick private residence in the city and one of the few of the Queen Anne style. It is now the home of George W. Jackson, son of Judge Jackson. Photograph courtesy of B.M. Hall.

This extant house on Mulberry Street was constructed in 1911. The prominent chimneys on the house in the right background identify the residence of John T. Dismukes on Water Street. To the right is one of the barns owned by Barling Grocery Company; half of the land-based warehouse was later incorporated into the extant Water Street residence of Harry Moore. Another warehouse was situated on the marsh between the mainland and the bay, sharing a common dock with the land-based structure. To the left is the house originally owned by the Barling family, later the residence of Colonel A. J. Sackett. Sackett sold the house to George W. Gibbs; it was razed in the 1970s. Photograph courtesy of Margaret Gibbs Watt.

The George W. Gibbs family relax on the porch in 1891. The house, located on the corner of Water and Locust streets, was the Gibbs' residence from the time of construction in 1875 until it burned in 1893. The encircling porch was incorporated into the design of many houses of this period, adding livability during the hot summer months. The porch posts exemplify a decorating custom of the nineteenth century, that of accenting the chamfers with a light shade of paint.

Gathered on the ground floor porch are: George W. Gibbs, leaning against a post; his wife, Margaret Watkins Gibbs, second from right; and Anna Everett standing behind the children, Margaret and George II. Elizabeth is on the bike and a nurse leans against the post. In the far corner of the balcony sits Harriet Everett. Julia (Mrs. George Couper) Gibbs stands behind her son, Robert Kingsley Gibbs. To their left is Emily Everett and Rebecca Gibbs with a doll. The Everett women lived at 28 Water Street and were among the first renters to lease from Lucy Abbott. Photograph courtesy of Margaret Gibbs Watt.

This 1885 bird's-eye view shows pre-Flagler St. Augustine. The Castillo de San Marco, right, marks the northern boundary of the colonial city limits with Abbott Tract extending beyond. The San Marco Hotel occupies acreage across Shell Road (San Marco Avenue), just north of the City Gate. In the center of the view is the plaza with the St. Augustine Hotel and the Cathedral on its northern border. The boat basin east of the plaza accommodates small crafts. St. Francis Barracks and the National Cemetery can be seen south of town, left on the sketch. Bridge Street received its name from the span crossing Maria Sanchez Creek, a body of water partially filled a few years after this sketch was drawn. The St. Johns River flows along the western boundary, top of the view. The lighthouse marks the tip of Anastasia Island. Drawing from the Boston Public Library.

Captain Richard H. Pratt spent three years in St. Augustine in charge of the Plains Indians confined at Fort Marion. Although townspeople were reluctant to permit an excess of freedom, they thrilled to the exhibitions and entertainment planned by Captain Pratt to raise money for education of the young. In time, a few Indians found employment in the city as Captain Pratt sought to teach some basic skills for later use in a complex society. The Army officer's humanitarian views led to the establishment of Carlisle Indian School in Pennsylvania. Photograph courtesy of Clarissa Anderson Gibbs.

Visitors from the Plains

Twice in about a decade, Fort Marion was temporary home to a unique and somewhat reluctant group of visitors. As the United States continued westward expansion, numerous rebel Indians were imprisoned in frontier forts. In May 1875 a group of these captives, consisting of Kiowas, Comanches, Arapahoes, and one Caddo, were shipped from Fort Leavenworth, Kansas, to St. Augustine. In charge was First Lieutenant (promotable) Richard H. Pratt, who arrived by train in the mid-summer heat with his shackled prisoners. Several suffered and died in the damp, hot environs of Fort Marion. Captain Pratt, however, showed compassion and wisdom in permitting a great deal of latitude in their activities. Soon the Indians were visiting Anastasia Island and eventually finding work within the community. A school established at the fort by local women was popular with the younger braves, if not the older men. For three years the Indians were separated from homes and families. When they were permitted to leave, in April 1878, most returned to the plains, although some accompanied Captain Pratt north.

In 1886 five hundred Chiricahua Apaches crowded into Fort Marion. They arrived in small groups, walking up Orange Street after days of travel in railroad cars. Geronimo's three wives were with the group, as was his sub-chief, Chatto. The notorious chief, however, remained a prisoner in Pensacola. One wife gave birth to a daughter during captivity. The infant was named Marion by the commanding officer, but later renamed Lenna by her mother. The Apaches, who were model prisoners, remained only a year. The school in the fort was reopened, and a few Indian children were permitted to attend school in town under the guidance of the Sisters of St. Joseph. Captain Pratt made several visits to select children for enrollment in his newly established Indian School in Carlisle, Pennsylvania.

Captain Pratt issued Army uniforms to the Indians. Photography from the Jacksonville Historical Society.

Indians make arrows during captivity at Fort Marion 1875-78. Photograph from Jacksonville Historical Society.

INDIAN SCHOOL AT FORT MARION.

Practical proof of sympathy with the red man has been shown by several worthy ladies, natives of or visitors in St. Augustine, Florida. In 1875, about eighty Indians belonging to various tribes whose agencies are in the Indian Territory were taken from Fort Sill to Florida, there to be kept as prisoners, under charge of Captain R. H. Pratt, of the cavalry service. Dirty, greasy, unkempt savages, loaded with chains, wrapped in their blankets, with the war-paint still soiling their faces, they have become, under the kindly treatment they have received, well-mannered soldiers in outward appearance, and inwardly, it is claimed for many of them, good, earnest Christians.

The lower illustration on page 373 shows the interior of the old Catholic chapel, in which to-day a class of Indian young men are being taught the simple knowledge of the Christian world, which it is hoped will turn their thoughts from the wild life they have heretofore led, and will stimulate them to an emulation of the best features in the life of the white man.

The old men do not care to attend the school, but the younger prisoners have become enthusiastic in their studies; so encouraging, indeed, has been the result of this primary teaching that benevolent persons have generously contributed sums of money for the furtherance of the good work, and this spring at least ten of the Indians are to begin their studies at some of the educational institutions of the North. The names of the teachers are Mrs. Couper Gibbs, Mrs. Kingsley Gibbs, Mrs. Caruthers, and Miss Mather.

In return for the kindness shown them by these excellent ladies, the Indians instruct them in archery, in the practice of which they are becoming very expert. The bow-and-arrow exercise takes place in the open court of the old fort.

Left:
This Harper's Bazaar *magazine article of May 11, 1878, praises the efforts of several women who strove to educate the Indians at Fort Marion. The teachers responsible for the successful school were: Sarah Mathers, Julia (Mrs. George Couper) Gibbs, Laura (Mrs. Kingsley) Gibbs, Amelia (Mrs. Horace) Caruthers, and Anna (Mrs. Richard) Pratt. Reproduction of article courtesy of the Independent Life Insurance Company.*

The Castillo (then called Fort Marion) was photographed from the San Marco Hotel in 1887. Sibley tents—Army tents supplied for use by the Apaches confined within the fort for a year—rise along the upper wall. Photograph courtesy of Charles Colee.

Three Apache Indians stand near a fort wall in 1887. Photograph from the Florida Photographic Archives, Strozier Library, F.S.U.

Sailing vessels grace the waterfront in this 1887 scene taken from the San Marco Hotel. Captured in the photograph is the city's oldest Protestant burial ground, commonly, though erroneously, called the Huguenot Cemetery. Records indicate the half-acre of ground occasionally served as a potters' field during the Spanish regime. The 1821 yellow fever epidemic created an immediate need for additional gravesites, and the lot became the final resting place for scores of Protestant citizens. In 1832 the land was deeded to the Presbyterian Church trustees. Descendants of the Kirby-Smith, Peck, Triay, Pacetti, and Manucy families are buried on the property. The last burial service occurred in 1884. Members of the church are currently restoring the historic spot. Photograph from the Library of Congress.

Neoclassical pilasters decorate the wall of the unfinished Spanish Treasury Building. This 1871 photo reveals a house behind the crumbling wall. From the Florida Photographic Archives, Strozier Library, F.S.U.

The Lorillard house was the winter residence of George Lorillard by the early 1880s. Lorillard, a member of the tobacco family, constructed his home in "stick style" Victorian architecture, reflecting the oriental motif inside and out. The St. George Street house was razed in the 1950s. Photograph courtesy of Albert C. Manucy.

The elegant San Marco Hotel, erected north of the City Gate, opened in 1886 as a major resort hotel for the city. Its existence was brief, however, ending in conflagration in 1897. Photograph from the St. Augustine Historical Society.

A walk along the seawall was a pleasant diversion in the 1880s. On the right, Capo's Bath House stands ready for bathers. Photograph from the Historic St. Augustine Preservation Board.

Charlotte Street and Baya Lane in the 1880s. Photograph from the Library of Congress.

This view of the Treasury and Charlotte Street intersection shows R. P. Sabate's store in 1886. The sign above the door advertises "Boots, Shoes, and Clothing." Photograph from the Library of Congress.

The plaza sometime before the fire of 1887. The St. Augustine Hotel, owned by Edward E. Vaill, looms above the Market Place. The hotel was never replaced after the conflagration; however, a reconstruction of the old Market Place now graces the plaza and represents the probable locations of markets as early as 1598. At that time, Governor Gonzalo Mendez de Canzo established a market on the plaza, initiating a system of standard weights and measures. Eighteenth-century documents indicate the presence of a guard house on the site, although it is believed the British (1763-83) operated markets on or near the present site of the Market Place. From the beginning of United States occupation (1821), structures on the plaza served as market places. Stories of a slave pen or slave market on the site are unfounded. A new market built around 1878 was probably located on Aviles Street, leaving the plaza structure vacant for auctioneers, public activities, and occasional loafers. Captain Vaill leased the old building in 1878, repairing the structure and decorating the plaza to the appearance in the photograph. Photograph courtesy of Margaret Gibbs Watt.

Above:
The Barcelona Hotel, constructed as a residence by Henry Ball in the 1870's, was originally located on Valencia and Sevilla Streets. In 1885, Henry M. Flagler purchased the structure and moved it north one block to Carrera Street. Modifications and additions produced the landmark hostelry which was razed in 1962. Photograph from the St. Augustine Historical Society.

Top:
The garden of the Magnolia Hotel provided a relaxing atmosphere for guests in the early 1900s. Located on the corner of St. George and Hypolita streets, the hostelry was erected by B. E. Carr in 1847. Soon enlarged to forty-five rooms, the house set a precedent for future guest accommodations in the city. In 1927 it was consumed by flames, the last of the massive wooden structures that predated the Flagler hotels. Photograph courtesy of Mr. and Mrs. Robert W. Harper III.

The St. Francis Inn has been continuously occupied since Gaspar Garcia built a coquina house on the property in 1791. Garcia maintained ownership until 1795, when the house and property were transferred to Rafael Saavedra de Espinosa. Its service as an inn began with the Dummett family, who moved into the house when forced to seek refuge from Seminole Indian attacks in New Smyrna. Thomas Henry Dummett, a former colonel of the British marines, died in 1839, leaving the property to his widow, Mary. In 1845 she conveyed the property to her daughters, Anna and Sarah, who opened a boarding house. When Sarah married Major General William Hardee, he became owner of the inn managed by the sisters, continuing the family business. It changed hands often after the Dummett-Hardee years and was renamed the Graham House while under the management and ownership of Thomas A. Graham (1925-1948). It is now owned by Mr. and Mrs. Charles Davis. Photograph courtesy of Mrs. Charles Davis.

The old stone watchtower of the first Spanish period was improved by the British with the addition of a signal gun, a retaining wall, and barracks. In 1824 an oil lamp converted the tower into a lighthouse. The site, however, proved to be unstable and is now completely submerged. Photograph from the Florida Photographic Archives, Strozier Library, F.S.U.

The present lighthouse, landmark of Anastasia Island, has been operational since 1874. It reaches a height of 162 feet with a beam visible nineteen miles over the water surface. Photograph from the Jacksonville Historical Society.

In the 1880s visitors crossed the marshland of Anastasia Island in the relative comfort of a horse-drawn railway car. A favorite stop was the lighthouse. Photograph from the Florida Photographic Archives, Strozier Library, F.S.U.

David Swain stands in front of the Coast Guard building at the base of the lighthouse during his first period as lighthouse keeper (1933-44). He donned the uniform when the Coast Guard assumed responsibility for Anastasia Light in 1939. After 1944 David Swain served in a number of lighthouses throughout the state. After retirement, he was asked to resume the position of lamplighter for the lighthouse and river beacons, a job he held until 1968. Photograph courtesy of Mary (Mrs. David) Swain.

St. Francis Barracks/State Arsenal

One of the structures abandoned by the Spanish in 1763 was the large bayfront building off Marine Street occupied by Franciscan monks. The coquina edifice, built about 1730, was situated in an area which documents indicate had been the site of a number of monasteries and convents since the 1500s. All previous structures burned or were destroyed by pirate attack or enemy siege. The L-shaped portion to the south and west of the Arsenal are the existing walls of the old Franciscan Monastery.

The advent of the British ushered in the military era for the building. British troops converted it into quarters and eventually increased its capacity with the addition of wooden barracks on adjoining property (now the National Cemetery).

Despite the return of the Spanish in 1783, the Franciscans never regained the building for religious purposes. Governor Zéspedes envisioned its usefulness otherwise, and Spanish troops were quartered in rooms vacated by British soldiers. The wooden structure burned in 1792, but the men continued living in the old monastery. When Spain ceded Florida to the United States, the Army immediately took charge of the barracks, issuing orders for repair in 1882. Ten years later St. Francis Barracks became a permanent military reservation.

The barracks served as a military post until 1900; however, seven years later it resumed its military function when the state of Florida leased the building as State Military Headquarters. In 1915 the structure was virtually destroyed by fire, leaving only the original walls intact. Since 1921, when Congress passed an act donating the barracks to Florida for military purposes, it has continued in this service. Renovated in keeping with the original St. Francis Barracks, the historic structure now houses the Headquarters Department of Military Affairs, state of Florida, and Headquarters Florida National Guard.

The earliest sketch of St. Francis Barracks/Florida State Arsenal was made in 1863. The appearance of the building has remained basically unchanged despite devastating fires requiring reconstruction. Drawing from Florida State Arsenal.

A review honors President Chester A. Arthur, who visited the Arsenal while in office (1881-85). Photograph from Florida State Arsenal.

Company C of St. Johns County Home Guards in 1918. Photograph from the Florida Photographic Archives, Strozier Library, F.S.U.

Chapter Five

The Flagler Era: 1888-1914

Henry Morrison Flagler (1830-1913) created an impact on St. Augustine unsurpassed by any other individual. Born in Hopewell, New York, the son of a Presbyterian minister, Flagler produced a fortune, primarily through his association with oil magnate John D. Rockefeller. In 1883 Flagler honeymooned in Florida with his second wife, Ida Alice Shourds. By the winter of 1885, Flagler was back with dreams of a Florida retirement spurring his interest in the state. Impressed by the potential of the ancient city, Flagler conceived the idea of developing a resort area with luxury hotels elegant enough to attract wealthy Northern families during the winter months. By January 1888 the Ponce de Leon Hotel opened, with the Alcazar rising across the street. Gradually transportation was improved, and the Flagler empire grew as St. Augustine entered its most exciting and prosperous era. Photograph courtesy of Clarissa Anerson Gibbs.

It required a man of infinite vision and abundant wealth to create the luxurious winter playground St. Augustine became. Henry Morrison Flagler was urged to visit Florida by the physicians treating his ailing wife, Mary Harkness. The extended stay in Jacksonville during the winter of 1878-79 did not include a trip to St. Augustine; however, Flagler witnessed the beneficial results of the healthful Florida climate as his wife temporarily regained strength. The desired return trip never materialized—Mary Harkness died in 1881.

Apparently Flagler was sufficiently impressed with Florida's warm winters to travel south once again, this time vacationing with his new wife, Ida Alice Shourds. Their 1883-84 winter honeymoon brought them to the quaint and mellow ancient city, and the seed was planted. Perhaps drawn by the cosmopolitan charm and unpretentious Spanish ambience, or lulled by the magic of the ocean breezes caressing the palms—whatever the reason, the millionaire oil magnate was compelled to return.

In 1885 the Flaglers traveled via the new Jacksonville, St. Augustine, and Halifax River Railway—a grueling, day-long trip, but an indication of progress. Immediately impressed with the changes wrought by the luxury hotel, the San Marco, Flagler pursued the dream that had germinated over the years. After a brainstorming session with Dr. Andrew Anderson, Flagler determined to construct an elegant hostelry which he would name the Ponce de Leon. Reputedly, the name was inspired by the elaborate celebration that year honoring Florida's discoverer.

Foremost in his planning was the selection of architects John M. Carrere and Thomas Hastings, and contracters James A. McGuire and Joseph A. McDonald. Together they produced the marvelous Ponce de Leon and Alcazar Hotels as well as the Presbytarian and Methodist churches and Flagler's home, Kirkside. Although McDonald continued working on Flagler's projects farther south, McGuire remained in the city building numerous residences and commercial structures.

Flagler's dream grew into an empire of

Kirkside became the winter residence of Henry Flagler in 1893. The Georgian Colonial house was razed in the 1950s. Photograph from the St. Augustine Historical Society.

hotels, railroads, resorts, and related projects to include agricultural development, civic improvement, and the erection of churches and hospitals. By 1888 the Ponce de Leon opened its doors to winter guests, with the Alcazar Hotel soon to follow. In 1889 Flagler bought the Casa Monica, renaming it the Cordova Hotel.

Transportation to St. Augustine had not been neglected by the entrepreneur. As early as 1885, Flagler had purchased the railway between St. Augustine and South Jacksonville. By 1888 his forty miles of track included the line from St. Augustine to East Palatka and the St. Johns Railway to Tocoi. Flagler now had access to the St. Johns River at two points, as well as control of a depot in Jacksonville. All that remained was to replace the ferry transporting passengers from the depot to the boarding site of the Jacksonville, St. Augustine, and Halifax line across the river. An all-steel bridge was completed in 1890, spanning the St. Johns, thus creating the final link between New York and St. Augustine. Within the ancient city Flagler erected a two-story depot on thirty acres of land beside the San Sebastian River. Winter visitors could now be appropriately accommodated upon their arrival in the resort town.

Additional developments directly related to the Flagler enterprises include the establishment of the town of Hastings (founded in 1890), and the growth of a residential area of St. Augustine known as the Model Land Company Tract. Prior to Flagler's arrival, the tract was a sparsely populated rural area nestled between the San Sebastian River and Cordova Street with Orange and King streets forming the north and south boundaries. In 1885 two estates occupied this area: Markland, belonging to the Andersons, and the Frances Ball house in the center of the quadrangle. A few

Christmas dinner around 1905 included, left to right: Mary Lily Kenan Flagler, Alice P. (Mrs. William R., Jr.) Kenan, Jessie Kenan Wise, Sarah Graham Kenan, nurse Janet Mitchell, Mary H. Kenan (mother of the Kenan siblings), and Henry Flagler. Photograph courtesy of Thomas Graham.

The women of St. Augustine honored Mary Lily Kenan Flagler, center, with flowers, during a formal ball in 1908. Guests included, left to right: Sara Barney (General Schofield's niece), Reginald White, and Captain H. K. Lyman. Ann (Mrs. W. A.) Knight and Mrs. R. N. Dickman stand in front of the column, and Sarah Lindsley sits in front of General Martin D. Hardin. Within the next group stand Fanny (Mrs. William W.) Dewhurst, W. A. Knight, Alice Macmillan Stewart, Mrs. H. K. Lyman, and Amelia Hardin (profile). Mary Smethurst stands behind, left (partially obscured) Major General John R. Brooks. Those in the front row to the right include Sarah Kenan, Mrs. G. M. Fletcher, Helen Miles (in dark-patterned dress), Jennie Lindsley, and Alford J. Thorn (white shirtfront). George F. Miles is pictured on the extreme right. Photograph courtesy of Clarissa Anderson Gibbs.

houses were clustered around the Catholic cemetery, and a small hotel, Sunnyside House, was located near the corner of present King and Cordova streets.

Collaborating with Dr. Anderson, Flagler purchased the Ponce de Leon site and several adjacent lots. By the early 1890s Flagler possessed the bulk of property included within the tract, with the exception of Dr. Anderson's estate and a few lots to the north. First to appear on the verdant acreage was Grace Methodist Church, followed by the magnificent Presbyterian Memorial Church and Kirkside, Flagler's own residence. Ancient City Baptist completed the quartet of remarkable structures. Soon after, spacious lots were parceled to wealthy winter residents, generating construction of elegant, commodious houses throughout the area.

Residents watched in amazement as the walls of the Ponce de Leon arose beside King Street, its grandeur and luxury surpassing the elegance of the stately wooden hostelries preceding it. Inspired by the Villa Zorayda, Henry Flagler employed the poured concrete method of construction and used a Spanish motif in keeping with the city's heritage. The interior was decorated by Louis Tiffany of New York; murals painted by George W. Maynard graced the dining hall and rotunda, and cherubs painted in Paris by Virgilia Tojetti stretched across the ceilings. The hotel, completed May 1887, probably looked like this 1889 photograph when the first winter guests arrived for the grand opening, January 10, 1888. Photograph from the Florida Photographic Archives, Strozier Library, F. S. U.

In 1903 thirty-seven acres of the tract were conveyed by Flagler to the Model Land Company, an organization incorporated in 1896 to handle Flagler's property acquisitions. Smaller lots were sold, and by the second decade the Model Land Company was primarily serving the employees of the Flagler enterprises, in particular those arriving to work for the rapidly expanding Florida East Coast Railway.

As St. Augustine reaped the benefits of Flagler's mighty empire, tragedy in the form of illness struck the millionaire's life once again. Alice Flagler lapsed into incurable insanity and was committed to a mental institution in 1897. After providing for her care, Flagler secured a divorce and married Mary Lily Kenan in 1901. They lived for a time in the ancient city, but Mary Lily desired a home of her own and a new environment—a dream fulfilled with the building of the palatial Whitehall in Palm Beach. The move was probably not difficult for Flagler since St. Augustine had proved somewhat a disappointment, never rising to his ambitious expectations. Glitter did not become the staid old city.

Flagler passed the remaining years of his life developing southern portions of Florida. He died in Palm Beach in 1913, and St. Augustine again felt the impact of the financial giant when a black-draped train returned the mortal remains to the city he loved. Businesses closed to mourn the death of the man who gave them the golden years. Henry Morrison Flagler was entombed in the mausoleum adjoining the Presbyterian Memorial Church where his first wife, Mary Harkness, daughter, Jennie Louise, and Jennie's infant already lay.

The courtyard of the Ponce de León in the early 1900s. Photograph courtesy of Thomas Graham.

Boston millionaire Franklin W. Smith was so impressed with Spain's Moorish palace, the Alhambra, that he chose to replicate one wing of the twelfth century castle and fortress. This he did in 1883, reducing the structure to one-tenth the original size and naming it Villa Zorayda after a daughter of the Sultan who had occupied the palace in Spain. The architecture and unique construction methods influenced Henry Flagler in the building of the Ponce de León Hotel. In 1913 Abraham S. Mussallem purchased the Villa Zorayda, adding his collection of valuable and rare furnishings obtained while serving as Egyptian consulate. In the 1920s Zorayda Castle operated as a gambling casino. Since 1936 the Mussallem family has maintained the building as a tourist attraction. Photograph from the Florida Photographic Archives, Strozier Library, F. S. U.

The Presbyterian parsonage was penned in 1884 for Chapain's Handbook of St. Augustine. *The St. George Street structure served as the manse until the Memorial Church and a new manse were erected by Henry Flagler. The Woman's Exchange occupied the building until it was razed for construction of the City Building, a Flagler project completed in 1896. Drawing courtesy of Margaret Gibbs Watt.*

The oldest Presbyterian Church in Florida was founded in St. Augustine in 1824 by Reverend William McWhir. Formal dedication of the coquina structure on south St. George Street took place in 1830. A second building, a chapel, was added in 1870 for evening services and Sunday School classes. It was later relocated on Cordova Street. Although occupied by Union Forces during the Civil War, the First Presbyterian Church served the congregation until Henry Flagler built the edifice in memory of his daughter. Eight coquina pillars surrounding Flagler Memorial were fashioned from the walls of the original house of worship. Photograph courtesy of Flagler Memorial Presbyterian Church.

Flagler Memorial Presbyterian Church

The tragic death of Jennie Louise Benedict stunned Henry Flagler, plunging him into profound grief. Seeking a fitting tribute to his beloved daughter, Flagler proposed the creation of a magnificent memorial church, an idea perhaps inspired by his deep religious convictions and family devotion. As a lifelong affiliate of the Presbyterian church, Flagler chose to approach the congregation of that denomination with an offer of a new house of prayer. The offer was quickly accepted, and Flagler's architects (Carrere and Hastings) and builders (McGuire and McDonald) commenced construction of the memorial. Soon the majestic Venetian Renaissance structure graced the city with its imposing grandeur, the only church of that architectural design in America. On March 16, 1890, Flagler family and friends joined with the Presbyterian congregation in a solemn dedication ceremony.

The Venetian-style copper dome of the church rises 150 feet from the center of the cruciform structure and is topped by a Greek cross ascending twenty feet higher. The base of the dome is ornamented with elaborate capitals of old-gold and white terra cotta. The pillars supporting the twenty-four arches are of red terra cotta, a theme continued in the red and old-gold terra cotta capitals of the four angle towers on the corners of the transept. The three Venetian arches of the front entrance lead into the magnificently furnished interior. Double cruciform bronze chandeliers hang from the high-vaulted ceiling. Brass Venetian torchiers overlook the rows of pews. The paneling, doors, and pews are carved mahogany from Santo Domingo; the floor is of imported Siena tile.

The Siena marble baptismal font is a gift in remembrance of Jennie Louise, given by her husband, Frederick H. Benedict. In 1902 Henry Flagler presented a series of stained glass windows representing the articles of the Apostles' Creed. Bronze doors and a marble archway lead from the nave into the mausoleum of the Flagler family.

Henry Flagler's home Kirkside was named for its proximity to the church he built. Photograph from the St. Augustine Historical Society.

Flagler Memorial Presbyterian Church, pictured around 1909. The round-domed mausoleum contains the sarcophagus of Jennie Louise Flagler Benedict with her infant, and of Flagler's first wife, Mary Harkness. After Flagler's death in 1913, he was entombed beside his family. A fourth stone coffin, intended for Flagler's son, remains empty, for Harry Harkness Flagler is buried in New York state with his immediate family. Postcard view from Florida Photographic Archives, Strozier Library, F. S. U.

Andrew Anderson (1839-1924) acquired his medical degree from the New York College of Physicians and Surgeons during the Civil War years, returning home in 1865 to twenty acres of prolific orange trees at Markland. He filled a void left after his father's death in 1839, administering the family estate and assuming civil responsibilities as had the first Dr. Anderson. Despite his Republican Party affiliations in a Democratic town, Anderson was elected city alderman in 1869 and 1875. During the 1870's he served three terms as county commissioner and in 1886 was elected mayor. His humanitarian sensibilities prompted his participation in the Buckingham Smith Benevolent Society and earned him a reputation as benefactor of the blacks in the city. As a practicing physician, he was aware of the health needs of the community and worked diligently to maintain efficient medical facilities in the Alicia Hospital and later the Flagler Hospital. He strove to establish a public school system and for fifty-nine years served on the board of trustees for the Presbyterian Church. When Henry Flagler visited St. Augustine in 1885, it was Dr. Anderson who sparked the flame of interest leading to the local development of Flagler enterprises. His concern for his birthplace spurred a consistent effort for improvement of the outward appearance of the town. His beautification projects included planting shrubs and trees and erecting public monuments such as the flagstaff outside the American Legion headquarters and the Ponce de Leon Statue at the foot of the bridge. The distinctive lions for which the span is named were a gift received by the city after Dr. Anderson's death. These, and numerous philanthropic projects, perpetuate the memory of this eminent citizen of the ancient city. Photograph courtesy of Clarissa Anderson Gibbs.

Left:
Mary Elizabeth Smethurst (1864-1912) married Andrew Anderson in January 1895. "Bessie" was the daughter of William Arthur Smethurst and Emeline Miller. After the death of his first wife, W.A. Smethurst married Mary W. Gibbs, beginning a bond between the Anderson and Gibbs families later strengthened by the marriage of "Bessie" Anderson's daughter, Clarissa, to Tucker C. Gibbs. Photograph courtesy of Clarissa Anderson Gibbs.

Markland, the Anderson family residence, was completed in 1841 on the twenty-acre farmland acquired by Dr. Andrew Anderson in the 1830s. Major expansion and renovation were accomplished by his son, the second Andrew Anderson, in 1900, bringing the residence to its stately appearance in this photograph, circa 1910. Now owned by Flagler College, it houses the William F. Blois, Jr., department of elementary and secondary education. The building was recently included in the National Register of Historic Places. Photograph couresty of B. M. Hall.

Alicia Hospital, named for Alice Flagler, was conceived in 1888 and made possible through the generosity of Henry Flagler and the labors of the St. Augustine Hospital Association. Dr. Andrew Anderson served as a board member for twenty-five years and was instrumental in establishing the new Flagler medical facilities after Alicia Hospital burned in 1916. Photograph from the St. Augustine Historical Society.

In 1902 these children gathered on the old rustic bridge in the Alcazar courtyard. From left to right: Georgene Dismukes, Hugh Lewis, Clarissa Anderson, Albert Lewis, Lillie Amy "Wiffie" Lewis, Andrew Anderson, and Georgena Schofield. Photograph courtesy of Clarissa Anderson Gibbs.

In January 1929 members of the group reunite with additions to the respective families. From left to right: Georgene Dismukes Mathewson with husband, Joe; "Wiffie" Lewis, Molly Lewis, Andrew Anderson III with wife, Roz, and daughter, Rozzie; Clarissa Anderson Dimick with husband, John. Photograph courtesy of Clarissa Anderson Gibbs.

The marble statue of Canova's Dancing Girl was a European purchase of Dr. Andrew Anderson, erected in the plaza to add a touch of old world charm. Unfortunately, children and vandals did not appreciate the beauty of the piece and the lovely lady was frequently damaged. The headless form now serves as an artistic pedestal beneath a shelf in the Rahner residence in Tampa. The identity of the piper is unknown. Photograph by H. M. Tucker; courtesy of Howard Hanson.

Sisters Alice Smethurst (Tyler) and Mary Gibbs Smethurst pose left and right, respectively, in this foursome. Mary Dewhurst (Blankenhorn) is seated in front of Elizabeth "Bessie" Frazer (Mrs. Reginald White) in this turn-of-the-century photograph. Courtesy of Clarissa Anderson Gibbs.

Olivet Methodist Episcopal Church was the first permanent place of worship for the Methodist Congregation of St. Augustine. No Methodist church existed in the city when hotel proprietors George L. Atkins and sons arrived from New Jersey. They organized a group which met in the Florida House during the winter season and in Liberty Hall in Government House (then the post office) during the summer. When asked to vacate the hall after two years, the group was invited to share the coquina church of the colored Methodists, an arrangement which continued until the erection of Olivet in 1874. This building was removed when Maria Sanchez Creek was filled. Photograph courtesy of B.M. Hall.

Members of Grace Church's first choir pose near the City Gate in 1888, the year Grace Methodist Episcopal Church (now Grace United Methodist Church) was dedicated. Grace Church, located on the corner of Carrera and Cordova streets, was built as the result of an agreement with Henry Flagler. Flagler wanted the land occupied by Olivet Church and parsonage. In return for that property, he built a new church and parsonage for the Grace congregation. The architects and builders responsible for construction of Flagler hotels and Flagler Memorial Presbyterian Church erected the structure for the Methodists. Photograph courtesy of B. M. Hall.

For about eight years the Baptists in St. Augustine worshipped without a church building or a permanent pastor. Learning of the congregation's difficulties, Henry Flagler offered the lot on the corner of Sevilla and Carrera streets with the stipulation that the building be erected within two years and cost less than $10,000. The stipulations were met and the first service held in 1895. This photograph, circa 1897, shows the Ancient City Baptist Church in its early appearance. Courtesy of Ancient City Baptist Church.

The garden of the Dr. Seth Peck House is shown here around 1937. The gently flowing arches and the molding on the capitals of the arcade columns revive the memory of Spanish days gone by. This home has the U-shaped "wing plan" of St. Augustine colonial architecture. There was an earlier structure on the site prior to 1690, but it was burned in the siege of 1702. Its masonry replacement was the residence of the royal treasurer, Don Estevan de Pena, until Florida passed into British hands in 1763, after which lieutenant governor John Moultrie lived here. Dr. Peck acquired the property in 1837 and added the frame second story. Photograph from the St. Augustine Historical Society.

Anna G. Burt, right, and Miss Chadbourne stroll through a garden. Anna was the granddaughter of Dr. Seth Peck, who immigrated to St. Augustine from Old Lyme, Connecticut. Miss Burt eventually inherited the family residence, living there for eight-one years. The home was conveyed to the city in 1931 through a bequest made in her will. Since Miss Burt was a charter member of the Woman's Exchange (founded in 1893), it was appropriate that the organization assume responsibility. The substantial house is interesting not only for its architectural attractiveness, but also for the collection of rare and valuable furnishings within. Photograph courtesy of the Woman's Exchange.

Flagler associate and brother-in-law, William R. Kenan, Jr., left, and land developer D. P. Davis converse on the golf course. Davis Shores on Anastasia Island was an innovation of the developer. Photograph from the Florida Photographic Archives Strozier Library, F. S. U.

Davis Shores, on the man-made extremity of Anastasia Island, extends from the Bridge of Lions northward in this 1970s view facing west. The Atlantic Bank building rises above the skyline at the city end of the span. The Castillo de San Marcos can be seen to the right, parallel to the tip of the Island. Photograph courtesy of the St. Augustine Record.

The clubhouse at St. Augustine Golf Links about 1920. The course was north of town, and a bus from the Ponce de Leon Hotel transported hotel guests and caddies. The clubhouse was built in 1915 by the St. Augustine Golf Development Corporation, a subsidiary of Florida East Coast Hotel Company. It was replaced in 1977 by the Ponce de León Country Club's new building. The course maintained twenty-seven holes until the 1930s, part of the lost playing area becoming the present site of the Ponce de Leon Lodge. In 1936 the St. Augustine Country Club, with golf pro Arthur A. Manucy, moved from their "little links" location to form the St. Augustine Links and Country Club. Photograph from the Florida Photographic Archives, Strozier Library, F. S. U.

In this rare action photo of golf as played in 1902, the woman's drive from the fifth tee soars safely left of the Castillo moat, a hazard that claimed many balls every year. The nine-hole layout of the St. Augustine Golf Club stretched between Riberia Street and the bay, and included much of the fort green. The course was used by local players and hotel guests from the latter 1800s until well into the twentieth century. The club, formed in 1898, operated from a clubhouse off San Marco, northwest of the Huguenot Cemetery. Another group, the St. Augustine Country Club, played on a nine-hole course south of town, known as the little links. Photograph from the Florida Photographic Archives, Stozier Library, F. S. U.

The no-longer-extant Florida East Coast train station around the turn of the century. The business offices were located on the second floor of the depot. Passengers boarded from a long shed, a portion of which shows to the right of the photo. The train then backed out of the station to continue its journey. Postcard view from Seth H. Bramson.

The pioneer railway connecting St. Augustine with the St. Johns River consisted of mule-drawn freight cars pulled along wooden tracks. Conceived by Dr. John Westcott, the little railway hauled its first passengers early in 1859. The fourteen-and-a-half-mile trip from Tocoi Landing to the San Sebastian River took three to five hours, often with repairs necessary along the way. By 1860 iron tracks and a steam locomotive replaced the cumbersome conveyance. However, during the Civil War the locomotive, parts of the track, and the Tocoi Depot were destroyed, and the line remained dormant for several years. Once revived in 1866, the line prospered and was purchased by William Astor in 1870. Rebuilt under his direction, the St. Johns Railway continued to function until purchased by Henry Flagler in 1888, when the line was incorporated into the Florida East Coast Railway system. Photograph from the Jacksonville Historical Society.

Electric streetcars transported passengers around the city from 1906-07 to the 1920's. Beginning at the northern city limits, the line extended down San Marco to the City Gate. Passing the fort, it continued down Bay Street to St. Francis, then down Marine to South Street, carrying fares to Flagler Hospital and Lewis Park Field. The trolley reached the King Street destination shown here by way of Central. A branch extended into West Augustine and another ran north on Malaga to the railway station. Photograph courtesy of B. M. Hall.

The wooden bridge to Anastasia Island was a welcome convenience when constructed in 1895. Pedestrians and bicyclists crossed for only five cents; toll for a double team and driver began at twenty-five cents, with an additional five-cent charge per person. The St. Johns Electric Company later laid tracks across the bridge, carrying passengers five miles down the island to South Beach. Postcard view from Seth H. Bramson.

In the 1880s passengers from Jacksonville were ferried across the St. Johns River to South Jacksonville, the boarding point of the Jacksonville, St. Augustine, and Halifax River Railway. Photograph from the Henry Morrison Flagler Museum.

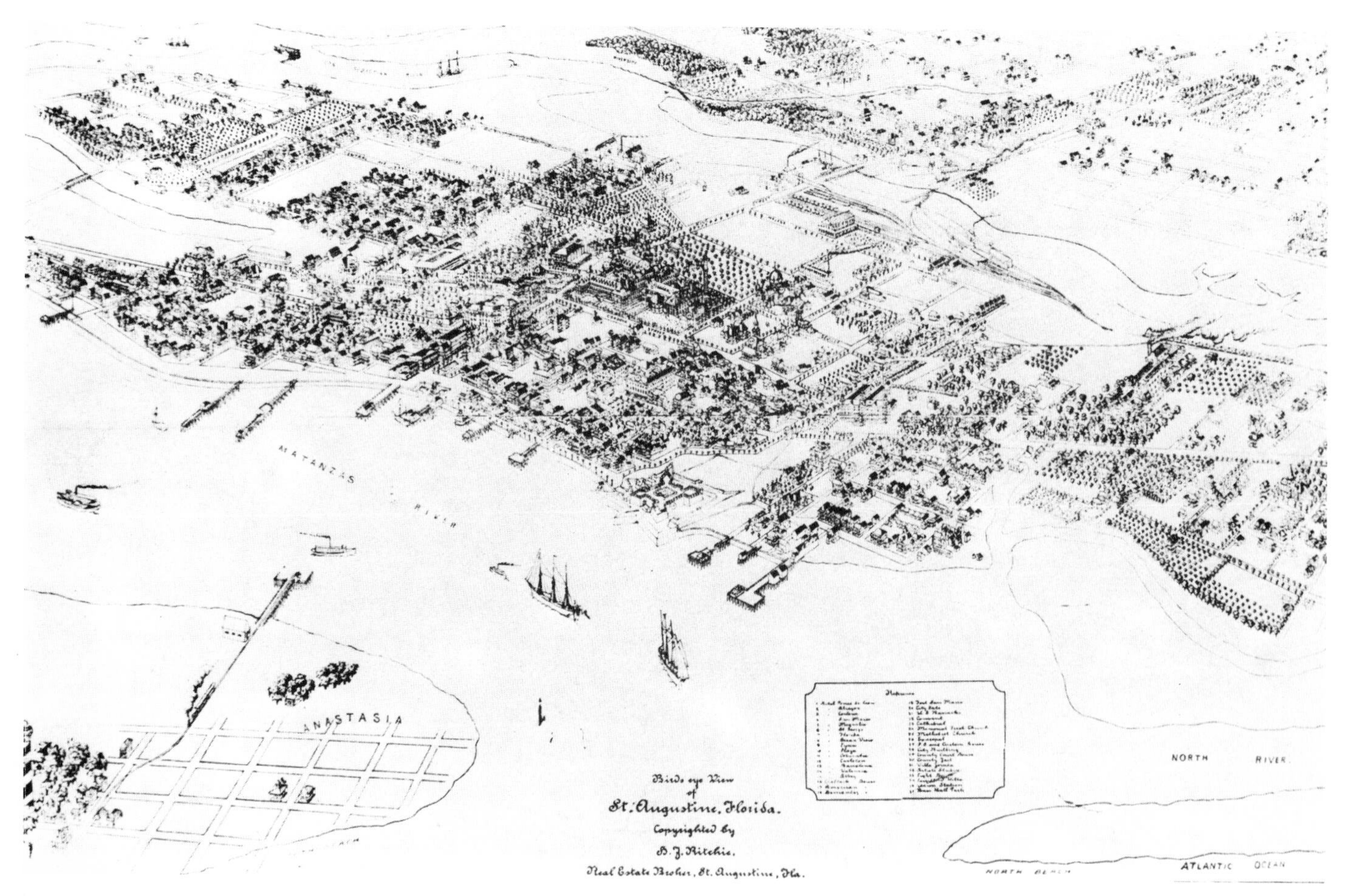

Numerous changes had occurred in the ancient city by the time this 1895 bird's-eye view was sketched. The impressive Ponce de Leon Hotel extends from King Street to Valencia, center, with the Cordova and Alcazar Hotels rising south, left, of King Street. Maria Sanchez Creek was filled for construction of the latter. The railroad depot and train station was built west of town, top, beside the San Sebastian River. The wooden bridge had not been built yet, and the ferry and steamtrain are pictured here serving Anastasia Island. A portion of North Beach appears at the bottom of the view, showing the passage for ships venturing into the ocean. Drawing courtesy of the St. Augustine Historical Society.

The Buckingham Hotel (no longer extant) on Granada Street is photographed here in 1916. It was initially created as a haven for destitute Negroes, supported by a bequest from Buckingham Smith. After Smith's death in 1871, a will was discovered in a safe at B. E. Carr's store (where patrons often secured their valuables). Since the bulk of the state was directed toward the care of the needy, an organization was established for the management of this and other charitable works. The Buckingham Smith Benevolent Association was formed by prominent citizens, including Dr. Oliver Bronson, his son, Oliver, Jr., Colonel John T. Sprague, James W. Allen, and Doctors Anderson and Peck. The organization has contributed its charitable works for over one hundred years. Postcard from the Florida Photographic Archives, Strozier Library, F. S. U.

Top Left:
The Jefferson Theatre stood on the corner of Cordova and Cathedral streets until 1955, when the St. Augustine National Bank purchased the property and razed the structure for construction of a new bank building. In 1967 the bank (renamed in 1971 the Barnett Bank of St. Augustine) extensively remodeled the structure. Photograph courtesy of B. M. Hall.

Top Right:
The Lyon Building, completed in 1887, occupies the corner of King and St. George streets. Today shoppers browse in Lyon Building stores much as they did in this 1910 photograph. Courtesy of B. M. Hall.

This 1962 view of 224 St. George Street shows one stage of development of an old St. Augustine residence. The building was first described on the Rocque map (1788) as a one-story masonry structure occupied by Juan Aguilar. Archeological evidence shows occupation on the site by early eighteenth-century Spaniards, and numerous artifacts prove residency in the house by the British (1763-83). In 1823 Bernardo Segui, the husband of Aguilar's granddaughter, borrowed funds presumably to add the second floor. Holmes Ammidown purchased the house in 1882, willing it after his demise in 1883 to his son, Henry Philip Ammidown. The Andrew T. MacMillan family moved to the house in 1885, leasing it for fifty years before assuming ownership in 1935. In 1963 the house was purchased by Rubye Lee and William K. Moeller, who are restoring it to its 1823 appearance. The stone wall to the left in the photograph marks the beginning of Palm Row property. Photograph courtesy of Mr. and Mrs. William K. Moeller.

The City Gate looked like this toward the end of the century when the roots of the cedar trees cracked the coquina. As city leaders contemplated removal of this memorial to the past, three spunky women demonstrated their disapproval. Elizabeth (Mrs. John) Dismukes, Annie (Mrs. Thomas) Woodruff, and Rosalie (Mrs. Josiah) James dressed in mourning clothes and, with black veils flowing in the breeze, served tea beside the wall until further consideration was given to saving the historic structure. Had it not been for their temerity, the City Gate might not stand today. Photograph courtesy of Margaret Gibbs Watt.

Right:
The quiet charm of Palm Row has attracted homeowners since its development in the early 1900s. During the 1870s through the 1880s Holmes Ammidown, a wealthy Massachusetts merchant, purchased considerable land along south St.George Street and built an elegant two-story house on land now the municipal parking lot. Before his death in 1883 he apparently inspired his son, Henry Philip Ammidown, to invest in adjoining property. Around 1910 six substantial houses arose between south St. George and Cordova streets. A common park was shared by the residents, and iron gates provided privacy for the tiny community. The land stayed in Ammidown family hands until 1941, when it was purchased by F. Charles Usina and W. I. Drysdale and sold by them to individual homeowners. It is apparent from this 1979 photograph that Palm Row has retained its delightful European character reminiscent of English mews. In. recent years the property has received attention from archeological discoveries; one of the digs uncovered a sixteenth century well, indicating the presence of homes near the Palm Row location around 1580. Photograph by Alec Mellon.

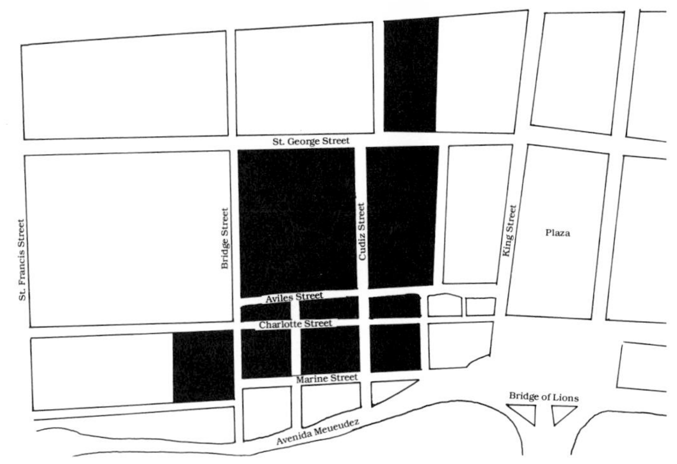

The location of Palm Row's sixteenth-century well is shown in the darkened area above (west of) St. George Street. Other dark sections indicate the probable areas of sixteenth-century occupation as discovered by recent archeological survey. A summer 1980 dig by archeologist Dr. Kathleen Deagan revealed the foundations of homes that may represent part of the earliest settlement in the United States. Author's sketch based on a map in The Archeology of First Spanish Period St. Augustine *by Kathleen A. Deagan.*

Crowds stood outside the fort in October 1905, during a visit by President Theodore Roosevelt. Photograph courtesy of Alma Clarke (Mrs. Robert L.) Fontaine.

A dredge chugs down the Matanzas River in 1910. Photograph by H. M. Tucker; courtesy of Howard Hanson.

Torpedo boats float peacefully in the bay during President Roosevelt's visit in 1905. Photograph courtesy of Alma Clarke (Mrs. Robert L.) Fontaine.

Treasury Street has the dubious distinction of being the narrowest street in the city, barely reaching a seven-foot width in some sections. Photograph from the Library of Congress.

The Vedder Collection of ancient maps and relics was exhibited by Nicholas Vedder in this Bay Street building on the corner of Treasury Street. The coquina structure was the former residence of John Leslie of the trading firm Panton and Leslie, which operated during the British and second Spanish regimes. The museum opened in the 1800s; the structure and its contents were consumed by flames in 1914. Photograph from the Florida Photographic Archives, Strozier Library, F.S.U.

The Ocean View Hotel, built in 1884 by William Slade Macy Pinkham, was located on Bay Street across from Pinkham's Dock. In 1909 the building was sold to H.E. Hernandez and was eventually razed in the 1960s. The site is presently occupied by the Marion Motel. Photograph courtesy of Slade D. Pinkham.

The City Gate at the turn of the century. The twenty-foot-high pillars are the only remaining portion of an elaborate system of fortification around the city. The northern entrance on St. George Street was constructed circa 1805 as part of the Cubo line, a defense wall extending from the Castillo to the San Sebastian River. Photograph from the Historic St. Augustine Preservation Board.

The Villalonga House, left, stands stripped of its balconies in this St. George Street scene, circa 1900. The wooden entryway on the right leads to the Lorillard Villa. Photograph courtesy of Mary La Verne Peck.

George Gibbs and his sister, Elizabeth Gibbs Weed, sail aboard their father's yacht, the Undine. *Their father, George Williams Gibbs (1853-1923), an avid yachtsman and the eldest son of Colonel George Couper Gibbs, served as a member of the city council. He was a banker and then general manager of Florida Coast Line Canal and Transportation Company. He married Margaret Watkins, whose father William J. Watkins, was twice mayor. She, too, served the community through the hospital auxiliary, welfare work, and various religious and social circles. Photograph courtesy of Margaret Gibbs Watt.*

Yacht racing reached a peak in popularity toward the end of the nineteenth century when white sails dotted the bay every winter season. In this 1902 scene sailboats gather in preparation for a race. Of the many sleek sailing ships, undoubtedly the most popular was the unbeatable Cheemaun, *owned and raced by W. S. M. Pinkham. Even the Andrew Carnegie sloop,* Misuse, *failed to best the* Cheemaun *in a two-boat race that delighted spectators in 1892. Photograph from the Florida Photographic Archives, Strozier Library, F. S. U.*

For many years the St. Augustine Yacht Club, shown circa 1904, operated from this bayfront building at the foot of Corbett's Dock, sponsoring races, regattas, and lavish dances for city residents and winter visitors. Formally organized in 1873, the club rapidly attracted prestigious Northern families. Membership rolls included names such as Colgate, Vanderbilt, and Stuyvesant. Henry Flagler's yacht, Adelante, *was often filled with guests watching the spectacular races. For sixty-seven years the club was the center of activity for boating enthusiasts. Now, after a lapse of almost four decades, it has been revived, and perhaps St. Augustine residents will again thrill to the sight of sleek racers skimming the water. Photograph from the St. Augustine Historical Society.*

Harris' Studio was one of many that flourished in the early 1900s. The cameras of Harris, Kugler, Blair, and Brown focused on faces of thousands of tourists and created lasting memories of the city. Caught before the lense are (from left): W.J. Harris, W.R. Hites, John G. Harris, unidentified, and Albert Cummins. From the St. Augustine Historical Society.

Frank B. Butler (1885-1973) was an active and dedicated member of St. Paul's A.M.E. Church, serving on the trustee board for fifty years. He operated the Palace Market on Washington Street and was president of College Park Realty Company. Butler Beach was named in honor of this man, who donated the property to the state for use as a park. Photograph courtesy of St. Paul's A.M.E. Church.

St. Paul's African Methodist Episcopal Church is pictured here in the early 1900s. The congregation was organized in 1873 by Reverend Richard James, who led the first services in a tiny building near Maria Sanchez Creek. In 1904 Reverend E.F. Williams organized the purchase of the lot on Central Avenue and was instrumental in building the church that stands today. Photograph courtesy of St. Paul's A.M.E. Church.

The Court House, photographed in 1902, was situated on the corner of Treasury and Charlotte streets. Destroyed in the 1914 fire, the brick building was replaced by a new structure by 1918. St. Johns County Court House is now located in the remodeled Cordova Hotel. Photograph from the Florida Photographic Archives, Strozier Library, F.S.U.

Blenmore, the residence of Charles Ferdenand Hamblen (1836-1920), is decorated for a 1907 Ponce de Leon celebration. Hamblen opened a business in St. Augustine in 1875. Originally a grocery store, the concern expanded to general merchandise and eventually specialized in hardware and building supplies. The Oldest Store Museum perpetuates the memory of the business and Hamblen's mark on the community. Photograph couresty of Michael Charles.

The Oldest Store Museum represents one of the oldest businesses in St. Augustine. The C.F. Hamblen Hardware Company started as a small mercantile concern. With the advent of the Flagler era, the entrepreneur from Maine expanded the business from groceries and general merchandise to include hardware and furniture. Groceries were dropped in 1888 as the hardware business developed. Around 1888 Hamblen moved his wares from a King Street location (present site of the Plaza Hotel) to Aviles Street. The museum occupies a building erected before World War I for use as a warehouse and garage for servicing vehicles; it has been in operation since 1961. The individuals in the 1880s costumes are, from left to right: Wiley Autrey, Carolyn Buell, Fred Green, and Shirley Green. Photograph courtesy of the Oldest Store Museum.

This structure on San Marco Avenue was the residence of William P. Genovar, the proprietor of the Cigar Emporium on St. George Street popular in the early 1902, about the time of the photograph. Courtesy of B.M. Hall.

Bartolo Thomas Genovar (1846-1945) holds the record for years of service on the Board of county commissioners. He chaired the board for twenty-four and a half years, giving a total of thirty-three and a half years to the county. Commended for his business abilities, Bartolo Genovar's reputation as successful merchant was widespread. Within the city he was a prosperous grocer and wine merchant with an interest in the entertainment field. His Opera House burned in 1914, but soon after he opened a theater on St. George Street which catered to traveling companies. In the county Bartolo experienced both success and failure. He owned a potato farm on land he named Elkton; however, his indigo business elsewhere did not prosper, nor did his pecan grove in a little town he named Bayard (for Senator Harry S. Bayard, an acquaintance). He was involved in numerous other ventures during his ninety-eight and a half years of life, including real estate and furniture. A newspaper article appropriately referred to Genovar as "the dean of early St. Augustine businessmen." Photograph courtesy of Eugenia Y. Genovar.

Ernest W. Howatt sits in his Stanley Steamer with his daughter, Gertrude, in 1907. His wife, Ida May, stands beside their Marine Street residence. Photograph courtesy of B.M. Hall.

The original wooden buildings of the Florida School for the Deaf and the Blind were constructed between 1883 and 1885 on property off San Marco Avenue. The founding date of 1885 dates this school as one of the oldest educational institutions in the state.

Senator Verle A. Pope holds a trophy presented in gratitude for his support of the Florida School for the Deaf and the Blind. He and school president William J. McClure stand before the Pope Vocational Building, named for the Senator's father. Verle Pope's parents, Artemas Winfred Pope and Cora Carlton Pope were the first two graduates of the school, receiving diplomas in 1898. Photograph courtesy of Margaret Pope (Mrs. Richard O.) Watson.

In 1902 Carcaba's Cigar Factory occupied this three-story structure on Cathedral Place. Formerly St. Mary's Convent and Academy, the building housed the first convent school in Florida, established by the French Sisters of Mercy in 1860. The bishop of St. Augustine gave the P. F. Carcaba firm use of the building after the cigar factory on Hypolita burned in 1895. At that time the cigar industry in St. Augustine was prospering, reaching a peak after World War I. By the 1920s the industry was the second largest employer in town, rivaled only by the Florida East Coast Railway. Photograph from the Florida Photographic Archives, Strozier Library, F.S.U.

City Hall, circa 1902, operated from the Municipal Building located on Hypolita Street between Spanish and St. George streets, a structure created through an arrangement with Henry Flagler. Flagler erected the building for city use, planning a market area, council chambers, and various city offices, including space for the police and fire departments and a prison. He offered the structure to the city for a very low rent with option to buy. The city market moved to the new accommodations in 1890, with the council members and fire department following in 1891. The U-shaped, three-story stone building housed municipal offices as well as the Model Land Company headquarters for many years. It was razed in 1973 by the St. Augustine Restoration Foundation. City Hall, the police department, and other municipal offices now operate from the remodeled Alcazar Hotel. Photograph from the Florida Photographic Archives, Strozier Library, F.S.U.

St. Cyprian's Church grew from the patience and determination of a small group of St. Augustine citizens who established an Episcopal mission in 1896. After several temporary locations, a permanent home was made possible through the help of winter resident, Emma (Mrs. Loomis L.) White. A series of fund raising events produced sufficient funds to erect the building shown here on Central Avenue in 1902. Photograph from the Florida Photographic Archives, Strozier Library, F.S.U.

Catherine Evans Usina cooks oysters on North Beach in the early 1900s. Photograph courtesy of Mary (Mrs. Francis) Usina.

St. Augustine's Beaches

As long as oceans and sand exist, sun worshipers and bathers will flood the shores. With the dawning of the 1900s, St. Augustine's beaches were discovered as a popular playground. An inlet divided the shoreline, creating two separate beaches for bathing pleasure: South Beach on Anastasia Island and North Beach on the southerly tip of a peninsula extending along North River. The Usinas and Capos developed North Beach, ferrying visitors across the river to pavilions, bathhouses, and oyster roasts. Henry Flagler brought guests more than once to Usina's Original North Beach. The Vanderbilt, Warden, Gould, and Lewis families dined on oysters cooked by Catherine Usina. A short distance south, Ellen Capo served clam chowder, chicken pilau, and all the fixings for twenty-five cents. City residents could visit either establishment and enjoy good food, fun, and a dip in the ocean.

In 1924 August Heckshers bought property on the south end of the peninsula, erecting the elegant Vilano Beach Casino in 1927. Unfortunately, the casino was eventually demolished after ocean waters encroached on the sandy foundations; however, entertainment was still available at Capo's and Usina's beaches. In 1938 Eunice Capo Banta purchased the Surfside Casino from her parents and continued developing beach property on the 165 acres owned by the Capo family. The Usinas' horse-drawn tram ceased operation in 1931, but the pavilion is still in use, now catering to the modern trend of family camping.

Before the beach boom exploded on South Beach, Anastasia Island lured visitors with other attractions. In the 1880s a ferry, *The Myth* transported passengers to the island, where they met a horse-drawn car that traveled part way to the lighthouse. Visitors could picnic and visit the ruins of the old Spanish beacon. By 1893 Felix Fire and George Reddington opened the Alligator Farm, operating a two-car steam engine from the ferry landing five miles to the farm and South Beach.

Visitors to Usina's Original North Beach enjoyed oyster roasts by the river, eating the delicacies under palmetto-thatched roof shelters amid orange trees. Scenes such as this in the early 1900s were frequent in the resort area. Photograph courtesy of Mary (Mrs. Francis) Usina.

In 1909 friends and relatives of the Usinas gathered alongside the North River for a roof-raising party, building the major portion of this pavilion in one day. For years dances were held and meals served inside the rambling structure. The St. Augustine city band often performed from a large porch called by some the bandstand. Today the structure serves as offices for North Beach Camping Park and as a social center for guests. Photograph courtesy of Mary (Mrs. Francis) Usina.

The wooden bridge, constructed in 1895, brought more traffic, and South Beach came into its own.

For years the Aspinwalls had been sole residents of the Island, but in 1907, nineteen names were listed in the city directory. Soon rental cottages were available for vacationers, and around 1908 a grocery store was established by Mary and Sepharin Busam on the corner of what are now White and Magnolia streets.

When the trolley (a replacement of the steam engine) ceased operation in 1930, swimmers migrated from South Beach to the more easily accessible Lighthouse Park area, where the municipal pier was ceremoniously opened in 1932 to accommodate the influx of beach enthusiasts. Over the years erosion and shifting sands have modified the shoreline. The municipal pier no longer reaches into the ocean, but extends over the silted waters of Salt Run. Swimmers travel south on the island to an access leading to beaches on a spit of land called Bird Island and Conch Island. Regardless of where the beaches lie, it is evident that sun worshippers and bathers will forever seek the sandy shores.

Visitors to North Beach traveled the one-third mile from river to ocean aboard horse-drawn trams such as this. The wooden bathhouses visible in the background burned in 1929, but the horsecars remained active on Usina's beach until 1931. An unconventional twist was the manner of hitching the horse; the animal pulled the tram from the side rather than the front. Because of the graded roadbed the trip to the beach was laborious, but the return was a breeze. Photograph courtesy of Mary (Mrs. Francis) Usina.

Ellen and Paul Capo sit in the famous trolley that carried passengers to their beach. "Uncle Sanchez" holds the reins. Paul Capo developed a pivot on a small platform beside the horsecar to facilitate directional changes at the termination of each trip. Photograph courtesy of Eunice Banta Bowen.

The Pauline II, *owned by the Capo family, is docked at its bayside pier. Photograph courtesy of Eunice Banta Bowen.*

During World War II servicemen from Green Cove Springs, Camp Blanding, Jacksonville, and the Coast Guard facility in St. Augustine gathered in the old city for weekend liberty. The Victory II *was permitted to use gas only to transport the soldiers and sailors around the bay at those times. The Usina family still operates the sight-seeing vessel on the bay. Photograph courtesy of Mary (Mrs. Francis) Usina.*

As early as 1912 a pilot found Capo's beach an interesting place to try his wings. On the left are the bathhouses for swimmers. The open pavilion (or lookout) is shown in its early form. Photograph courtesy of Eunice Banta Bowen.

This photo, circa 1922, shows the casino and pavilion. The top floor of the casino was used for dancing; the bottom consisted of bathhouses and showers. The buildings on the left are the first group of houses built on North Beach. Photograph courtesy of Eunice Banta Bowen.

For years alligators have intrigued both tourists and Florida residents accustomed to the creatures. In 1893 Felix Fire and George Reddington capitalized on this interest, opening the Alligator Farm and Museum of Marine Curiosities on a site near Anastasia Island's Salt Run, the location pictured here. Apparently the "burning spring" on the farm was equally alluring; visitors traveled the two-car steam engine to view the fiery mixture of gas and water as well as the giant reptiles. The farm prospered on this site until erosion necessitated a move inland, somewhat farther north on the island. Ocean waters now cover the former home of the alligators. In 1937 W. I. Drysdale and F. Charles Usina purchased the farm, adding alligators from a Jacksonville attraction. The marshland denizens continue to lure visitors to their habitat, which now includes the additional appeal of Ross Allen's Reptile Show. Photograph courtesy of St. Augustine Alligator Farm.

Right:
The palatial casino on North Beach opened in 1927. It was constructed by August Hecksher, owner and developer of Vilano Beach. The casino boasted a large swimming pool, 150 feet long and 50 feet wide. The ballroom was a masterful replica of Spanish art, drawing accolades for its antiquated cypress ceiling with rustic beams, the oversized fireplace, and lush drapes. However, even the money of the New York investor could not keep the sea from claiming the resort as its own. The ocean washed away the beach and the bulkheads during the 1930s until water met walls, necessitating demolition of the remaining structure by 1938. Drawing courtesy of Mary (Mrs. Francis) Usina.

VILANO BEACH CASINO

Three bathers enjoy a day on the beach around 1925. Photograph courtesy of Ellie Shepherd (Mrs. Roscoe) Pomar.

Beach atire has changed over the years, but so has the concept of "bathing." The quiet Anastasia Island beach pictured here normally abounds with swimmers and surfers. Photograph by Randy Hoff.

Ocean play around 1910. Photograph courtesy of Mary La Verne Peck.

Anthony Vincent "Bossy" Monson, around 1912, was proprietor of the Monson Hotel. The Monson name, originally spelled Osmunson, came from Norway. The first family member born in St. Augustine was William Osmunson born in 1815. Photograph courtesy of Mary La Verne Peck.

The Octagon House was constructed in 1886, a late edition of the 1850s style popularized by Orson Squire Fowler, a prominent phrenologist, lecturer and amateur architect. The extant structure served as a summer cottage at the time of this photograph in 1910. Photograph courtesy of Jean Pomar Hoey.

The old Wireless Station used by the Coast Guard in the early 1900s now is a residence near Lighthouse Park. Photograph courtesy of Jean Pomar Hoey.

Center House, owned by John L. Center, Sr., was rented by visitors to Anastasia Island. It was washed away during a storm around 1910. Photograph courtesy of Jean Pomar Hoey.

The Monson Hotel was erected on Bay Street to replace the original Monson House, a late nineteenth-century wooden structure that extended from Charlotte to Bay streets. The hotel, built after the 1914 fire destroyed its predecessor, was razed in the 1960s. The Monson Motel now occupies the site. Photograph courtesy of Mary La Verne Peck.

Fritchieff Monson (1849-1904) stands beside his catch of three large drum. The man to the left is unidentified. "Fritchie" operated the ferry over the San Sebastian River from 1865 to 1867. The "ferry" was an inelegant rowboat that functioned until a wooden bridge was constructed in 1871. Photograph courtesy of Mr. and Mrs. Russell Mier.

The St. Augustine Transfer Company operated initially from this Cathedral Street location, shown around 1910. The Colee family has provided carriage service to St. Augustine since the 1880s, when Louis A. Colee formed the business. In his day several types of carriages were required, including Landaus used for funerals. Essentially, it was a taxi service, conveying passengers between the railroad depot and hotels. With the advent of automobiles, the prudent Mr. Colee converted the rigs to sight-seeing vehicles. Visitors to the city delight in riding through the streets in the open carriages, and for years the horses have played a prominent part in the annual Easter Festival. Photograph courtesy of B. M. Hall.

Cathedral Street around 1912. Photograph courtesy of Mary La Verne Peck.

A popular thoroughfare in 1907 was old Horn Road, where this photograph of Lula Alba Pomar was snapped. In present times, following Horn Road would involve a trip up Route 1, a westward turn to Masters Drive, a southward route on Masters to Evergreen, and a little jog on Palmer to reach King. Photograph courtesy of Jean Pomar Hoey.

The marsh of Maria Sanchez Creek lay along the west side of St. Augustine and militarily was a natural defense in colonial times. However, when the Flagler hotels were built, much of the upper creek bed was filled. Then the causeway and dam shown in this 1910 picture were constructed across the creek at South Street, impounding its waters into a small lake. Photograph courtesy of Jean Pomar Hoey.

Two women enjoy climbing in the magnificent live oaks of Garnett Grove. The famous orange grove was planted by Dr. Ruben B. Garnett shortly after his arrival in St. Augustine around 1883. Photograph by H. M. Tucker; courtesy of Howard Hanson.

A corner of the Magnolia Hotel, left, overlooks the Pojoud House in 1912. The house is architecturally significant, representing early nineteenth-century construction. It is historically interesting because the property was once owned by the fascinating Francisco Xavier Sanchez and his wife, Maria del Carmen Hill Sanchez. Now owned by the Independent Life Insurance Company, it opened in 1969 as the Sanchez House, exhibiting a variety of museum pieces. Photograph courtesy of the Independent Life Insurance Company.

Assuming the role of Ponce de León was a serious undertaking for Harold W. Colee in 1925. For each pageant, two men were selected to portray Ponce de León and Pedro Menéndez, the city's founder. Photograph by Victor Rahner; courtesy of Prime Beaudoin.

Ponce de León Celebrations

The traditional celebration of the "landing of Ponce de León" began in the 1880s with parades, regattas, fireworks and festivities lasting two or three days. In 1890 Governor Francis P. Fleming marched with Mayor W. S. M. Pinkham down Bay Street, leading colorful floats, two batteries of U.S. artillery, and scores of school children and residents. A 1907 celebration was plagued by inclement weather, resulting in destruction of the caravel built to convey Ponce de Leon and his retinue to shore. Apparently the rain did not dampen the spirits, for the boat was repaired and the festivities continued a few days later. The pageantry was maintained throughout the 1920s; however, depression days brought an end to the activities that delighted residents and attracted visitors to the ancient city.

Celebrations commence with the landing of the Spanish caravel carrying Ponce de León and escorts—historically inaccurate, but fun nevertheless. Photograph by P. A. Wolfe; courtesy of Lily Golden Hogle.

Hundreds of spectators watch the 1908 pageantry depicting the confrontation between a Spanish landing party and the Indians. Photograph courtesy of Earl L. "Ike" Masters.

A few liberties are taken in the re-enactment of attacks on the fort, but the action thrills spectators. Photograph by P. A. Wolfe; courtesy of Lily Golden Hogle.

Opposite Page:

Pirates represent the attacks of Drake and Davis. Photograph by Victor Rahner; courtesy of Prime Beaudoin.

The finance committee delegated to raise funds for the Ponce de León celebration of 1907 were, left to right, standing: Ernest Mahr, W. S. M. Pinkham, Frank Howatt; seated: Eugene Masters and A. M. Taylor. Photograph courtesy of Slade D. Pinkham.

The joint committee in charge of the 1907 Ponce de León celebration included, left to right, standing: City Marshal W. E. Hinch, F. J. Howatt, Harry Rogero, J. Herman Lynn, Charles F. Hopkins, Jr., Harvey Tomlinson, W. S. M. Pinkham, Antonio Entenza, Fred A. Henderich, J. L. Henry, Robert P. Kettle, Eugene Masters; seated: E. I. Leighton, A. M. Taylor, A. W. Corbett. Photograph courtesy of Slade D. Pinkham.

Mill Creek School was one of several that opened in St. Johns County around 1879. This sketch depicts the first of four structures built to educate the community children. "School Number Seven" opened in January 1879 with eighteen pupils attending. The structure burned in 1893 and was quickly replaced by a similar one-room school. Another school was contructed in 1913, but it was 1927 that marked the beginning of a new era for education of local children. Mill Creek School, Consolidated, was constructed for the benefit of students from Picolata, Switzerland, Bakersville, Sampson, Race Track Road (near Bayard), Hardwood, and Orangedale. Now fifty years old, the school still serves a large portion of northwestern and western St. Johns County. Drawing by Hiram F. Ortagus.

The Public School System

Until 1835 education in the city and county was generally administered by tutors, private schools, or church-affiliated organizations. Efforts to establish free public schools failed miserably, usually due to apathy or nonavailability of qualified instructors. In 1831 the Florida Educational Society was formed in Tallahassee, but produced no significant change in St. Augustine. A school opened in 1832, but was forced to close when taxpayers refused monetary support. It was the bequest of Charles Lawton in 1835 that led to educational opportunities for children of poor families in the town. A trust fund channeled through the city council gave religious leaders financial aid to provide schooling for qualified students. In 1868 a formal public school system was made possible with financial assistance from the Peabody Fund. The Peabody Free School Committee was formed in 1868, resulting in the Peabody Fund School for white children and the Peabody Fund School for black children.

Schools in outlying county areas evolved after the school laws of 1869 became effective. By 1877 twenty-four white and colored educational facilities were scattered throughout the county; most were small and primitive. In 1879 School Number Seven was established off Pacetti Road with Mary Ludwig as teacher and Thomas A. Pacetti as superintendent. Although the one-room log schoolhouse burned, it was replaced in 1893 and again in 1914. Through these buildings, the current Mill Creek School can claim one hundred years of continuous public education.

Teachers in the public school system often started their careers in the small country schools. Maude Shorter, a public school teacher for forty-eight years, began at Bakersville. Christian Bonfield, Gertrude Speissegger, and Leone Roode all gained experience in the county schoolhouses. Teachers normally boarded with local families on a monthly basis and were paid about fifteen dollars a month.

The superintendent and teachers of the St. Augustine public schools are pictured in 1912. Left to right, bottom row: Aileen Cooper (Gates), Hazel Brandt, Mabel Haigler (Rice), Pauline Gatchell, Ada Coughlin (Williams); second row; unidentified, Professor C. A. Keith, Superintendent W. S. M. Pinkham (1901-1912), Evelyn Hamblen, unidentified; third row: Isabella Hopkins (Hawkins), Gertrude Speissegger, unidentified, Laura P. Hawkins, and Mrs. Annie M. Averette; top row: unidentified, Maude Shorter, Agnes Coughlin (Copeland), Leone Roode, Kathleen Pitts. Photograph courtesy of Slade D. Pinkham.

A public school class around 1907. The wooden school building on Artillery Lane and Aviles Street can be seen in the background. Left to right, back row: unidentified, Robert Crutchfield, Ansley Canfield, Amos Corbett, Harry Snow, unidentified, unidentified, Walter Henry, unidentified, Slade Pinkham, Mier Tarlinksi; second row from top: Emery Simms, Edna Nelson, Thera Speer, Leonora —, Ida Mae Cook, unidentified, Dorothy Milburn, unidentified, Leroy Scott, and Harry Pinkoson; kneeling, second from left, Ray Faver. The others are unidentified. Photograph courtesy of Slade D. Pinkham.

By the early 1900s the little brick schoolhouse on Hospital (Aviles) Street, including its wooden additions and annex, was bursting its seams. A new building was petitioned, and in 1909 Orange Street School was completed. Within fifteen years, it, too, was inadequate to meet the needs of a growing population. A high school (later junior high) was built in 1924 and named Ketterlinus for Elizabeth B. Ketterlinus, a Warden daughter who donated the land. The growth spurt of the 1920s necessitated the construction of other facilities throughout the county to include Fullerwood, Hastings, Mill Creek, and Evelyn Hamblen schools. In the 1950s a new crop sprang up, consisting of John A. Crookshank, Hastings High School, R. B. Hunt, Richard J. Murray, Ponte Vedra-Palm Valley, and James A. Webster. St. Augustine High School followed with completion in 1960. St. Augustine Technical Center began classes in 1970 in St. Augustine High School, moving to new facilities on Collins Avenue the following year. By the end of the decade enrollment for day school, night classes, and the adult-general division was more than eight thousand. Students from St. Augustine High School, Hastings High School, and St. Joseph's Academy may attend vocational classes at the center for part of each regular school day if desired.

In total, the greater St. Augustine area contains seven elementary schools, a junior high, a high school, and one vocational-technical center. St. Johns County claims two elementary schools, Julington Creek and Ponte Vedra-Palm Valley (both kindergarten through ninth grades), with Hastings contributing an elementary school and a high school (seventh through twelfth grades). Enrollment in the public school system for the 1978-79 school year approximated eight thousand. Students wishing to obtain higher education locally can apply to Flagler College, a private, four-year liberal arts school.

Right:
The Orange Street School class of 1930-31. Left to right, standing: Wallie Huff, George Jackson, William Justice, Eugene Capps, Harold Gunnells, Billy McGuire, Jack Broudy, Nelson Reichardt, Earl Truett, Maude Shorter; seated: Benjamin Dunton, Carl Wakely, Jaime Cacaris, Eugene Wasson, Virgil Hartley, Douglas Hartley, Margaret Tedder, Peggy Ann Pierce, Virginia Pitts, Leonora Hopkins, Caroline Barrett, Louise James, Debora Smith, Helen Greene, Erma Cubbedge. Photograph courtesy of Alma Clarke (Mrs. Robert L.) Fontaine.

Right:
The St. Augustine High School basketball team during the 1922-23 season. Left to right: Davies Meitin, Worth Gaines, Frank Howatt, Clifford Earls, Arthur Manucy, Earl Masters, Amadeo Meitin, Verle Pope. William Abernathy, seated, was coach. Photograph courtesy of Earl L. "Ike" Masters.

Orange Street School has changed little since this photograph taken shortly after construction in 1909. St. Johns County's oldest school still in use is now being phased out to be replaced by a new elementary school in the southern part of the county. Photograph courtesy of B. M. Hall.

Founded in 1963, Flagler College created an academic atmosphere within the walls of the former luxury hotel, the Ponce de León. The four-year liberal arts college maintains an enrollment of approximately seven hundred students. Photograph courtesy of Flagler College.

Built in 1924, Ketterlinus educated high school students until 1960, when the present St. Augustine High School was constructed. Ketterlinus served as a junior high until 1970, when it was converted to an eighth and ninth grade center under the county grade-center plan. The lower grade was transferred to Murray Seventh Grade Center. Photograph courtesy of Historic St. Augustine Preservation Board.

St. Augustine High School, on Lewis Speedway, was completed in 1960. Enrollment by the end of the 1970s reached approximately 1,250. Photograph by Robert Lange.

The disastrous fire of 1914 started in the boiler room of the Florida House shortly before one a.m., April 2. Flames swept across the heart of the city, greedily devouring four hotels, the Courthouse, the Opera House, and countless homes and businesses. Surviving buildings border the charred wasteland from St. George Street to the bay. Miraculously saved, the wooden Magnolia Hotel, left, faces the coquina Pojoud House (now Sanchez House) that stands unscathed with its white walls denying the damage of the night. Behind the residence rise the walls of the Municipal Building, from which the fire department was called to battle the nightmarish flames. Photograph courtesy of Mary La Verne Peck.

Chapter Six

Twentieth Century Growth

The death of Henry Morrison Flagler marked the close of an era of opulence, but not the end of progress in the tourist town. After recovering from the tragic 1914 fire—a conflagration which destroyed the heart of the city—St. Augustine experienced a period of growth and development unprecedented in its three-and-a-half centuries of existence. While the world was at war, Florida's potential was realized, largely by the numerous military men encamped throughout the state.

By 1919 Florida's boom years were well underway, and, although St. Augustine was only on the fringe of the phenomenal real estate explosion, it was not excluded from the 1920s growth spurt. The population almost doubled between 1920 and 1930, reaching more than twelve thousand. This was partially due to the expanded city limits in 1924, although the growth was essentially real. This can be compared to the 1978 figure of 12,611.

The decade of the twenties brought the shrimp industry to St. Augustine. The business became the fourth largest industry in the county by the 1940s, providing employment for more than four hundred fishermen.

Land developer D. P. Davis, who won fame and fortune in Tampa building a community on previously submerged land, attempted a similar venture in St. Augustine, filling the salt marsh of the northern extremity of Anastasia Island. Work began in 1924, and by 1927 at least a dozen families lived on the 395 man-made sites. About this time, the bubble burst in Florida. His company declared bankruptcy and Davis disappeared at sea shortly thereafter. Thompson-Ryman realtors purchased the assets, selling individual lots to prospective home builders. However, it was not until after World War II that Davis Shores realized its full potential.

Tourism remained the principal economic mainstay of the community, a fact appreciated by Dr. Andrew Anderson, who concentrated the efforts of his waning years in beautification of the city. In addition to the flagpole in front of the American Legion Building, Anderson contributed

St. Augustine citizens of the twentieth century were chosen to portray sixteenth century Spanish heroes at the 1926 Ponce de León celebration. Ponce de León (James A. Colee, center left) and Don Pedro Menéndez (Edward E. Warwick, center right) are surrounded by their captains in this souvenir program. Courtesy of B. M. Hall.

the Ponce de Leon statue on the east end of the plaza and the noble lions at the foot of the bridge. Tourism, still essential to the city's economic stability, has continued to flourish. In 1978 321,311 visitors viewed the historic town.

Growth was reflected also in the construction of the enormous First National Bank Building (now Atlantic Bank Building) on Cathedral Place. The structure was completed in 1928, shortly after the Bridge of Lions was opened.

In the early 1940s a new industry was introduced into the city. Diesel Engine Supply Company (Desco Marine) was founded in 1941 by Jacksonville industrialists Leo C. Burgman and L. C. Ringhaver. By the end of the 1970s the company had launched over two thousand wood-hulled

The Segui Bookstore, located in the burned-out Lynn Building, was fully restored in this 1916 photograph. Behind the counter is Maud (Mrs. Charles D.) Segui. Her daughter, Martha Lee, left, stands with her cousin Michaelina Arnau. To the right is Charles D. Segui. The bookstore, in operation from 1907 to 1945, carried the largest selection of newspapers in the city, serving Northern visitors living in hotels such as the Magnolia down the street. Students remember Mr. Segui as the city's authorized school book dealer. Photograph courtesy of Martha Lee Segui.

Sunlight bathes the smoldering ruins of the Monson House after the 1914 fire. Photograph courtesy of Mary La Verne Peck.

shrimp boats and had branched into production of fiberglass vessels; it employed more than seven hundred workers. Atlantic Yacht Corporation and St. Augustine Trawlers joined the boat building industry in the 1970s. The Trawlers, established in 1971 by Jerry Thompson, found steel hull protection profitable as well as the conventional wood and newer fiberglass boats.

For nearly two decades Fairchild Industries employed city and county residents, maintaining a payroll of up to six hundred persons. The airplane assembly plant closed in 1976.

Progress also entails a concern for undeveloped land and reassurance that improvement under the guise of progressiveness will not ravage the countryside. At least two men personally guaranteed the availability of acreage for recreational use. Frank B. Butler donated a strip of land extending from the ocean to the inland waterway as a park, at the time intended primarily for use by the black community. In 1950 Hiram Hall Faver gave the state seven hundred acres of land in the southern part of the county for the use as a state recreational park. The park is a memorial to his parents, Alexander Hall Faver and Florida Ellen Dykes Faver.

Some fascinating research has been conducted in this decade under the auspices of Florida State University and the Historic St. Augustine Preservation Board. Much has been learned about the ancient city through archeological excavations begun in 1972. The theory

Children pose outside the "University of Moccasin Branch" in the early 1900s. The school was an integral part of St. Ambrose parish, the Catholic pastorate of Father Stephen Langlade. Arriving in St. Augustine in 1871, Father Langlade focused attention on the county communities of Bakersville and Moccasin Branch. He constructed the St. Ambrose Church in Moccasin Branch in 1875 and arranged for the Sisters of St. Joseph to open a school for the Catholic children. Twenty-seven students attended the first classes in 1881. By 1892 seventy-eight pupils were enrolled, but the need for a twelve-year school was rapidly declining. By 1905 it was reduced to the elementary levels (grades one through nine). The St. Ambrose school continued to educate the youth of the parish until 1948, when the final class of sixteen students prepared to enter the Hastings public school system.

Left to right, bottom row: Theodore Triay, Henry Williams, Wilbur Simms, Ambrose Masters, Phillipe Masters, Madison Bennett; second row: Antonia Sanchez, Barbara Williams Wakely, Risha Williams Masters, Hattie Sanchez, Estelle Triay Masters, Elaine Cody Higgenbotham; third row: "Sudie" Maxwell, Christina Masters Sanchez, Alice Solano, Sister Ambrose, Mae Triay Masters, Marcella Masters Triay. Photograph courtesy of St. Ambrose Parish.

proposing that early settlement was south, rather than north, of the plaza was tested and confirmed. Evidence of a sixteenth- to seventeenth-century residential structure was uncovered on the corner of Charlotte Street and Bravo Lane. Two sixteenth-century wells discovered on the Trinity Episcopal Church site and a Palm Row site clearly indicate the existence of houses in that area around 1580. All evidence supports the theory that the founders of the ancient city put down roots in an area of about nine blocks south of the plaza, roughly bordered by Marine, Bridge, and St. George streets.

Perhaps the most significant event of the twentieth century was the recognition of St. Augustine's importance as "a national history sanctuary"—a phrase conceived by the late President John F. Kennedy. In the 1930s the Carnegie Institute of Washington, D. C., proposed an endowment for the restoration of the ancient city. The National Committee for the Preservation and Restoration of St. Augustine, Florida, was formed in 1936. The ensuing research led to the development of plans which unfortunately were abandoned at the outset of World War II.

A resurgence of interest occurred in 1959 when the Historic St. Augustine Preservation Board was established with the support and direction of Senator Verle Pope and Governor LeRoy Collins. The state-sponsored preservation board has accomplished far more that the town and county could have achieved alone. The eighteenth-century character of colonial St. George Street exemplifies their work.

Restoration, preservation, and research are essential in maintaining the historic integrity of this ancient city. St. Augustine has been labeled unique, quaint, and, of course, old. It has been called a city of contrasts and a cosmopolitan conglomerate. Indeed, it is all of this. It is a special place: a sleepy but bravely tenacious garrison town; a settlement plagued by misfortunes, never ambitious but never conceding defeat. It is the cradle of Christianity in the United States and, most importantly, it is our nation's oldest city.

Our Lady of Good Counsel Church was dedicated in Bakersville in 1902. The church was originally built around 1875 as St. Leopold Church in Mill Creek, but it was determined that Bakersville was a more suitable site for the parish church. The building was relocated by dismantling St. Leopold Church in Mill Creek and restoring the structure to its original style and size. Photograph courtesy of Our Lady of Good Counsel Church.

St. Johns County Development

Created by an ordinance in 1821, the 39,376-square-mile area of east Florida shared with Escambia the distinction of becoming the first counties of the state. Rapidly diminishing in size as new counties were formed, St. Johns dwindled to the 609 square miles it contains today.

A few settlements dotted the countryside long before Florida became a United States territory. In 1736 a wealthy Spanish cattle rancher, Don Diego de Espinosa, maintained a fortified hacienda on coastal property north of St. Augustine. Originally built as a defense against Indian attack, Fort San Diego was later manned by Spanish soldiers and eventually captured by General James Oglethorpe when he led an expedition down the narrow peninsula toward St. Augustine. Reputedly, Diego de Espinosa was a native of the Spanish city Ponte Vedra, thus giving the area its name.

The little community of New Switzerland, on the St. Johns River, was founded by Swiss native Francis Philip Fatio, Sr., who built a country estate on ten thousand acres received as a land grant during the British regime (1763-83). The plantation buildings burned in 1812, but the community survived, passing into the capable hands of Fatio's daughter, Louisa Fatio, who administered her holdings from St. Augustine. Elegant homes now dot the riverside in this northern corner of the county.

In 1804 Andres Pacetti II received a Spanish land grant of 604 acres in what is now the Bakersville area. He built a house, establishing his family on property still inhabited by Pacetti descendants. Around the same time, Bartolo Solano settled on land farther south, naming it Moccasin Branch. By 1830 the United States government granted to Solano 640 acres of land which he and family members strove to develop. In the western portion of the county George Colee and his wife, Tryphena Riz, homesteaded in Picolata. A short distance south on the St. Johns River, the tiny community of Tocoi arose, with settlers Paul Weedman and his wife, Antonia Rogero, assisting in the development. These early pioneers withstood the threat of Indian attacks and later bore the hardship of isolation during the Civil War.

In the 1870s a new settlement was founded by Captain Lewis Coxetter. Originally named for the steamboat captain, the town of Bakersville attracted colonists from South Carolina, including: Dr. Thomas Speissegger, Dr. John C. Ludwig, W. R. Lee, and families Appler, Powers, Hertz, Starowski, Mahr, Coler, Daigle, Klipstine, and Hawkins. This enterprising band of settlers produced crops, grew orange trees, and raised farm animals. The logging business prospered as the colonists learned to float cedar, pine, and cypress logs down Deep Creek (Six Mile Creek) to the St. Johns River, where they were towed to Jacksonville. In addition to the numerous sawmills sprouting around the county, cane grinders were a common sight, squeezing juice from sugar cane to boil into molasses. This industry was no doubt responsible for the appellation Molasses Junction, bestowed on the settlement by John Rogero.

An unusual county resident was composer Frederick Delius (1862-1934), who purchased an orange grove in 1884 at Solano Grove near Picolata Landing. Through friendship with the Anderson family, the musician was introduced to folk and Negro spirituals indigenous to northeast Florida. The music of *Appalachia*, the *Florida Suite*, and the opera *Koanga* reflect this influence.

The 1870-80s also saw growth through the efforts of Father Stephen Langlade, the Catholic priest who erected two churches, a rectory, a convent, and a school serving the settlements from Mill Creek to Holy Branch (Spuds). The core of the county was no longer a frontier. The influx of settlers infused vitality into the sparsely populated countryside as newcomers worked with the native families of Solanos and Pacettis, and the Weedmans, McConnells, Taylors, Ashtons, and Bells.

One county community virtually disappeared. Evaville—population fifty—contained a post office,

Composer Frederick Delius (inset) was a young man when he resided in his cabin near Solano Grove around 1884. Drawing and photograph from the St. Augustine Historical Society.

The Weedman family sit on the porch of Bartola Weedman's Bakersville house, circa 1910. Left to right: two of Bartola's daughters, Frances and Bertha, unidentified child, Albert Weedman, daughter Nettie Weedman Pacetti, and Bartola Weedman. Photograph courtesy of Charley Sanchez.

This 1916 photograph was taken in front of Louis Pacetti's house, built on ten acres of land given him by Domingo Pacetti, Sr. The property was a portion of the original land grand acquired by Andres Pacetti II in 1804. With Louis is his wife, Susie Lowe Pacetti, and baby Martha; seated at left is Theresa Paffe, a relative through the Hernandez side. Photograph courtesy of Lorna Pacetti Ortagus.

For a pleasant summer vacation, St. Augustine families and friends could take a two-hour wagon ride to Moultrie and a comfortable farm house overlooking the Matanzas River. Here the women could bathe in the shallow water while the children made friends with Mr. Harrison's horse, Toby, and his flock of geese. The photograph was snapped by Art Manucy in 1914 on such an outing. Left to right: Elizabeth (Mrs. Arthur D.) Manucy, Mr. and Mrs. Harrison, Albert Manucy, an unidentified couple, and Grace (Mrs. Daugherty) Bridier. Photograph courtesy of Albert C. Manucy.

a school, and a newspaper called the *Datil Pepper*, published by the town's founder, Lewis W. Zim. Zim migrated from Louisiana in the 1880s settling in an area on Trout Creek four miles east of the St. Johns River. Naming the new community for a daughter, Zim lived and worked in the county town until the turn of the century, when he moved to St. Augustine. The agricultural community simply disappeared after that, presumably due to difficulties following the 1890s freeze that destroyed the orange crop.

Two agricultural towns did root firmly in county soil: Hastings, developed to grow produce for Flagler Hotels, and Elkton, a farm town named for the Benevolent Order of Elks by property owner Bartolo Genovar.

As potatoes and cabbages flourished in the county's interior, the somnolent strip of beach property known as Diego witnessed a revival. First families of the beach community included the Micklers, Thomas Oesterreicher, Joe Jones, Eli Broadnax, William DeGrove, Kit Lowe, the Miers, the Hensons, and Thomas Patton. The name was changed from Diego to Palm Valley shortly after 1906, and the Intra-coastal Canal, dug about 1908, brought new life to the isolated settlement. The sandy soil did not inspire rapid development, but today the resort community of Ponte Vedra Beach includes the historic Palm Valley region as well as the newly created Sawgrass, Innlet Beach, and De Leon Shores developments.

Another rapidly growing resort area is St. Augustine Beach, located south of the ancient city. The seaside community reached a population of 1,131 by the end of 1978. Although the population of the ancient city has remained stable during the 1970s (12,352 in 1970 and 12,611 in 1978), the county has increased its number from 31,035 to 44,550 in the same time frame. Hastings remains around 620, a figure it has retained for at least two decades, while the unincorporated areas reflect recent growth with the current figure of 30,188, an increase of 12,776 since 1970.

Marcus D. Pappy rests on the sugar cane piled in his cart as daughter Ocia looks on. The photograph was snapped on the Pappy farm in Sampson around 1915. Courtesy of Eulalia Walker Langston Compton.

This old still bubbled its brew in St. Johns County during the early 1900s. Photograph by H. M. Tucker; courtesy of Howard Hanson.

Thomas Horace Hastings, a distant cousin of Henry Flagler, gave his name to the settlement he founded about eighteen miles from St. Augustine. Photograph courtesy of the town of Hastings.

Main Street, Hastings, in 1926. Hastings, the Potato Capital of Florida, was founded in 1890 at the suggestion of Henry Flagler. Fifty men moved with their families into makeshift cabins on the new experimental plantation. A railroad was established, and the farm town began producing vegetables primarily for the Flagler hotel system. By the 1920s agricultural advancements made large-scale potato farming a reality with shipments soon filtering to states throughout the country. Photograph courtesy of the town of Hastings.

The J. B. Hughes Building on Boulevard, now Main Street, in Hastings. The structure contained grocery and dry goods stores of the merchant for whom it was named. Photograph courtesy of Shirley Sanchez Browning.

A horse and buggy are decorated for the opening of Dixie Highway in 1914. The horse, Teddy, was owned by C. A. DuPont. Ethel DuPont and Alma McCullough McLoud help celebrate the occasion. Photograph courtesy of the town of Hastings.

In 1916 travelers on Old Dixie Highway made the trip over bricks, as did the passengers and driver of this Studebaker. Photograph courtesy of the St. Johns County Extension Service.

DuPont Stables in Hastings operated on the present site of the Hastings Potato Growers Association. It was owned by C. A. "Gus" DuPont, who eventually turned his stable into a theater for silent movies. The conversion was made around 1914 and lasted until the building was destroyed by fire in 1919. A pool room adjoined the theater and was probably as popular as the silent screen stars who played their parts to the accompaniment of "Professor Carter's" piano. Photograph courtesy of Jean Pomar Hoey.

Hastings citizens gather around a wagonload of full potato barrels. Among those pictured in this 1916 photo are: Fred Flake, C. A. DuPont, Fred Kaiser, Bob Emerson, Louis Levine, Reverend Seading, Wofford Campbell, C. H. Campbell, Mr. Taylor, J. G. R. Smith and C. A. Campbell. Photograph courtesy of St. Johns County Extension Service.

The first mechanical potato digger was used by Littlefield and Erwin Company on this Hastings farm in the 1920s. Photograph courtesy of St. Johns County Extension Service.

Above:
Women cut seed potatoes in Hastings around 1916. The potatoes were shipped from the north, cut in quarters, and planted for the next crop. Photograph courtesy of St. Johns County Extension Service.

Top:
George W. Waller, in white hat, center, raised cucumbers as well as potatoes on his farm. Photograph courtesy of St. Johns County Extension Service.

In the fall of 1947 a schooner was wrecked on Ponte Vedra Beach during a severe northeaster. The ribs of the vessel are visible at low tide less than a half mile south of Mickler's Road. The sea accident is reminiscent of another incident in the vicinity, the landing of four Nazi saboteurs in 1942. Disembarked from a German U-boat, the agents buried explosives and journeyed north, where they were eventually captured and executed. Photograph courtesy of Pete Hopkins.

This 1964 view shows a Switzerland home on the St. Johns River. Photograph courtesy of the St. Augustine Record.

A 1970s view of Ponte Vedra Beach shows the growth of the resort area. Houses dot the lagoons and inlets that lie between the shore and highway A-1-A. Our Lady Star of the Sea Catholic Church borders the highway, right foreground. Photograph courtesy of the St. Augustine Record.

In DuPont Center, a crossroad on U.S. Highway 1 and Route 206, scenes such as this were routine. Willis Joe Capo, back to camera, George E. DuPont, and Donnie DuPont feed sugar cane into the mill in this early 1950s photo. The juice is collected in barrels and cooked until it reaches the appropriate consistency for syrup. Photograph courtesy of Donnie DuPont Gadar.

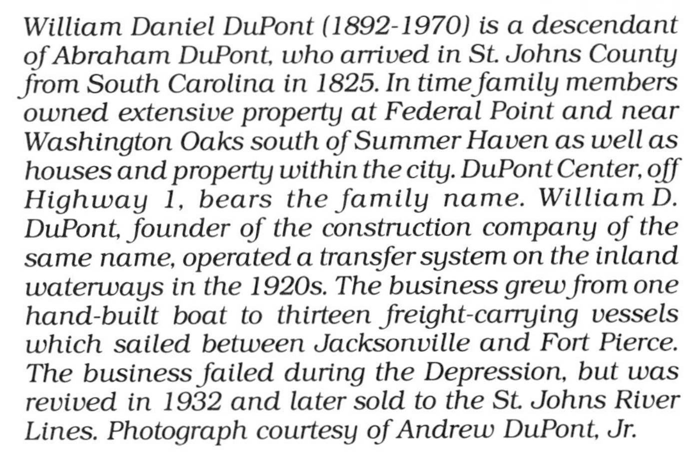

William Daniel DuPont (1892-1970) is a descendant of Abraham DuPont, who arrived in St. Johns County from South Carolina in 1825. In time family members owned extensive property at Federal Point and near Washington Oaks south of Summer Haven as well as houses and property within the city. DuPont Center, off Highway 1, bears the family name. William D. DuPont, founder of the construction company of the same name, operated a transfer system on the inland waterways in the 1920s. The business grew from one hand-built boat to thirteen freight-carrying vessels which sailed between Jacksonville and Fort Pierce. The business failed during the Depression, but was revived in 1932 and later sold to the St. Johns River Lines. Photograph courtesy of Andrew DuPont, Jr.

Sea Crest Inn, left, a popular Summer Haven resort, is shown here around 1920, when it was built by Virgil DuPont Bryant, the son of proprietors James M. Bryant and his wife, Alice Virginia DuPont Bryant. The Bryants occupied the small building on the right, operating a post office there around 1912-19. The hotel was sold in 1924 to the Mellon family, who ran the hostelry as Cove Tavern Inn and have resided in the structures ever since. Photograph courtesy of Alec Mellon.

Hunting for deer, turkey, and squirrels as well as quail and dove in St. Johns County was both popular and productive. These hunters proudly pose with a fine buck. Photograph courtesy of Eulalia Walker Langston Compton.

The construction company of B. B. McCormick builds a road (A-1-A) from Ponte Vedra to St. Augustine in the 1930s. Now an exclusive resort, Ponte Vedra was once torn by dredges digging for minerals needed during World War I. The National Land Company scraped the beaches for zircon, silicate, monozite, titanium, and other ores. Development of the resort community began about 1928 when a log clubhouse and nine-hole golf course were constructed. Popularity spread, and by 1937 a new facility, The Inn, was built to accommodate beach visitors. Photograph from the Beaches Area Historical Society.

William Arthur MacWilliams (1863-1952), born in Camden, New Jersey, made a significant contribution to St. Augustine and the state of Florida. His legislative career began with membership in the Florida House of Representatives in 1899. He was an elected official to both the House and Senate for a total of thirteen terms, the last in 1935. During the 1921-22 term he served as president of the Senate. He was one of the organizers of the Florida State Bar Association, holding office as president at one time. As an officer in the Florida National Guard, he achieved the rank of brigadier general and was the adjutant general in 1901, the year of the tragic Jacksonville conflagration. He was a practicing attorney in St. Augustine, forming partnerships with George Bassett, P. L. Perry, Claude G. Varn, and Frank P. Upchurch, Sr. The William A. MacWilliams Law Library in St. Johns County Court House perpetuates the memory of his legal pursuits. An avid golfer, MacWilliams played often with Warren G. Harding during the President's visits to the city. He was instrumental in permanently locating the Florida School for the Deaf and the Blind in St. Augustine, an ever-present reminder of this man's devotion to people and his city. Photograph courtesy of Polly (Mrs. Peter) Pierce.

Gertrude de Medici MacWilliams (1866-1937) managed well her role of wife and hostess for her senator-general husband. At one time she entertained William Jennings Bryant as a house guest. Her roots were deep in St. Augustine as a descendant of one of the New Smyrna colonists. Her ancestor, Elias Medici, was a shoemaker from Corsica. The oldest son of Elias Medici and his wife, Tecla Marin, was born in the ill-fated colony in 1773. A 1783 census shows Elias living in St. Augustine as a widower with three children. Photograph courtesy of Polly (Mrs. Peter) Pierce.

President Warren G. Harding (pin-striped suit) during one of his visits to St. Augustine, possibly 1921. Photograph courtesy of Thomas Graham.

President Harding arrived in St. Augustine on the yacht Victoria, *shown here in front of the Monson Hotel. Photograph courtesy of Thomas Graham.*

In 1923 the Jewish congregation of St. Augustine built on south Cordova Street, a house of worship, a brick-walled synagogue with a commanding stone facade and elegant stained glass windows. The First Congregation of B'nai Israel was organized in 1904 by a handful of men led by Jake Tarlinsky. Charter members included: Isaac and Max Eff, Morris Friedman, Nichols Gamse, David Mehlman, William A. Pinkoson, and Saul A. Snyder. Snyder, a native of Russia, was a well-known cattleman and rancher who resided in Fernandina when the prayer group was formed. He and others from the area moved to St. Augustine to unite with members of their faith. Photograph courtesy of the St. Augustine Record.

A band concert, circa 1924, in the plaza. Photograph courtesy of Earl L. "Ike" Masters.

Mable (occasionally spelled Mabel) Cody was the first woman to attempt a speedboat-to-plane transfer, the boat-to-plane change was performed over Vilano Beach in 1924. Her plane was a standard J-1, piloted by Slim Culpepper. This same act is currently demonstrated by Colonel Moser's Air Circus in St. Augustine. Photograph by H. M. Tucker; courtesy of Howard Hanson.

Mable Cody's superb airshow thrilled St. Augustine audiences with daring stunts and precision flying. The pretty pilot from Birmingham, Alabama, feared nothing as she performed with her Flying Circus. Here her plane taxies down the beach in July 1925. Photograph by H. M. Tucker; courtesy of Howard Hanson.

This 1928 photo probably marks the introduction of ethyl gasoline. Harry S. Rowe stands beside his truck on Hartshorn Street in West Augustine. Photograph courtesy of Geraldine Rowe Maguire.

Roscoe Pomar and shop owner Curtis D. Peele pause from work in Nelmar Sundries around 1927. Peele operated the store on the corner of San Marco Avenue and May Street for eight years, offering the first curb service in the city. Photograph courtesy of Ellie Shepherd (Mrs. Roscoe) Pomar.

George W. Corbett's fish market operated at the head of his dock on the bayfront. Photograph by H. M. Tucker; courtesy of Howard Hanson.

Senator A.M. Taylor holds his daughter, Edith, in 1906. The senator served in the Florida legislature from 1925 to 1931. Photograph courtesy of Margaret Pope (Mrs. Richard O.) Watson.

Edith Taylor Pope (1906-61), daughter of Senator A.M. Taylor and Florence Tugby Taylor, was the author of numerous novels, including two with Florida settings, River in the Wind *and* Colcorton. *Her political associations were transferred from her senator-father to her husband, Senator Verle A. Pope. Photograph courtesy of Margaret Pope (Mrs. Richard O.) Watson.*

James Draper Ingraham holds Leonora Douglas Stoddard in 1940. Ingraham, a passenger agent for Florida East Coast Railway, was the son of James E. Ingraham, one of Henry Flagler's chief agents responsible for the St. Augustine enterprises and president of the Model Land Company. Photograph courtesy of Leonora Hopkins Stoddard.

First cousins, Leonora Margaret Hopkins and Isabella Gibbs Ingraham unveil a plaque on the Post Office building in 1922. Charles Floyd Hopkins, grandfather of the two cousins, was St. Augustine's Postmaster from 1915 to 1924. His son, George Couper Gibbs Hopkins, looks on from the doorway. He assumed the position of postmaster in 1945, serving until 1959. Photograph courtesy of Leonora Hopkins Stoddard.

The Gibbs and Hopkins families are represented in this 1979 photograph by cousins Margaret Gibbs Watt and Doctor George Couper Gibbs Hopkins, Jr. Margaret Gibbs Watt is a descendant of Colonel George Couper Gibbs, who was born in St. Augustine in 1822 shortly after the Gibbs family immigrated to Florida from North Carolina. George Hopkins traces his lineage to Indian agent Colonel Gad Humphreys, also of the territorial period. Humphreys' grandson, Charles Floyd Hopkins, married Isabella Barksdale Gibbs, thus uniting the Gibbs and Hopkins families. Dr. Hopkins was the first pediatrician in St. Johns County, opening practice in 1950. He established and headed the first pediatric unit at Flagler Hospital and was the physician for high school athletic activities at the Florida School for the Deaf and the Blind for about twenty years. Photograph courtesy of Leonora Hopkins Stoddard.

Tucker Carrington Gibbs (1889-1965) in Naval dress around 1920. An Annapolis graduate, Tucker traveled around the world, including China, where his sister, Margaret, met her husband Albert W.J. Watt. While in his native city Tucker assumed the family sense of community responsibility, serving on the board of trustees of Flagler Hospital, as warden of Trinity Church, and as supporter of the Red Cross program and public school system. His marriage to Clarissa Anderson formed a second bond between the prominent families of Anderson and Gibbs. Photograph courtesy of Clarissa Anderson Gibbs.

The Bridge of Lions under construction in 1927. The old wooden bridge on the right remained operational until the official opening of the new span, April 7, 1927. Photograph by H.M. Tucker; courtesy of Howard Hanson.

This lion and his marble mate have guarded the city side of the Bridge of Lions for more than half a century. Photograph from the St. Augustine Historical Society.

The Bridge of Lions adds a touch of old world charm to the bayfront as it links Anastasia Island to the ancient city. Dominating the skyline at the foot of the span is the Atlantic Bank Building, constructed at about the same time as the bridge. Completed in 1928 for the First National Bank of St. Augustine, it was vacated the following year when the bank failed. For ten years the structure served as a warehouse, mercantile store, and temporary post office. The Exchange Bank acquired the building in 1939 and has maintained ownership since. The bank name changed to Atlantic in 1970. Photograph from the St. Augustine Historical Society.

Florida East Coast Railway's baseball team in 1925. Left to right, seated: Reuben Masters, Phillip Flautt, Ernest Hall, Ralph Bolick; center row: Elzie Masters, Merrill Wolfe, Fred Bolick, Russell Frilp, Earl Bussey, Worth Gaines; back row: Earl "Ike" Masters, William Thompson, Pierce Evans, Noel Mier, Francis Carriss. The photo was taken in Lewis Park. Photograph courtesy of Earl "Ike" Masters.

The St. Augustine City Commission of 1928 included, left to right: V.J. Mickler, C.A. Lamont, Mayor Frank D. Upchurch, Elwood Salmon, and Thomas Walker. In addition to mayoral duties, attorney Frank Upchurch was politically active as a state representative for Nassau County in 1921 and state senator for district 31 in 1943. Photograph courtesy of Frank D. Upchurch, Sr.

Smoke and flames engulf the Magnolia Hotel on St. George and Hypolita streets. Although the fire department occupied the west wing of the City Building directly across from the hotel, the structure was destroyed. This aerial view was taken by pilot R.S. Campbell, December 27, 1926. Photograph courtesy of B.M. Hall.

The St. Augustine Fire Department is pictured here, circa 1910, outside its headquarters, the wing of the City Building bordered by Hypolita and Spanish streets. Prior to 1900 the fire department consisted only of volunteers. By the time Elwood Hartley (later chief) joined the city-created force in 1921, there were four men, a five-hundred-gallon pumper, and a fire wagon drawn by two horses named Dick and Harry. Hartley was a fire-fighter for forty-one years and was succeeded as chief by B. M. Hall in 1963. Photograph courtesy of B.M. Hall.

The St. Augustine Fire Department, circa 1948. Left to right, front row: Chief Elwood Hartley, Carl Mickler, D. Menser, Frank Lewis, T. H. Nelson, Edsel Manucy, Amos McCormick, B. M. Hall; back row: Herbert Capo, Rufus Stratton, Roderick Hartley, Sub Strickland, J. V. Davis, D. W. Borum, Leon Desvousges. Standing in the entrance is Birtie Masters. Photograph courtesy of Earl L. "Ike" Masters.

The St. Augustine Police Department in 1910. Photograph courtesy of the St. Augustine Police Department.

Virgil Stuart, left, was Acting Chief of Police in 1949 when this photograph was snapped on the fort green. Frank Copeland stands at right. The modern vehicles were an improvement over the touring models (including Model-A Fords) used when Chief Stuart joined the seventeen-man force in 1934. Photograph courtesy of the St. Augustine Police Department.

Police Department

Until 1885 a town patrol maintined law and order—and kept the cows off the streets. When this system was deemed inadequate, a uniformed police force was established, consisting of a captain, one sergeant, and three policemen. Apparently the quiet town lived a peaceable existence until 1910: the 1904 city directory notes only one additional patrolman, but the captain and sergeant were then called marshall and deputy marshall; by 1910, however, the department had increased to a total of then. Now, sixty-nine years later, the expanded force consists of six dispatchers and more than thirty officers.

The three pioneers of shrimping were all immigrants from Italy who arrived in Fernandina Beach in the early 1900s. Salvatore Versaggi (top), Anthony Poli (center) and Sollecito Salvador (bottom) moved their business to St. Augustine in the 1920s as the shrimping industry grew in economic importance in the life of the communtiy. By the late 1940s there were one hundred ships operating out of St. Augustine, and shrimping ranked as the fourth largest industry in St. Johns County. Photographs courtesy of Nelli Poli Caruso and Hon Versaggi.

Unique to Spanish-oriented St. Augustine was this windmill, part of the Dutch Tavern on Anastasia Island. Located near the foot of the Bridge of Lions, the restaurant served the public from 1937 to 1955 under the ownership of Joseph X. Ponce. Later, as Norman's Windmill Restaurant, this touch of the Netherlands played a feature role in a Route 66 *television series. The building no longer exists. Photograph courtesy of James A. Ponce, Sr.*

One of the newest vessels built by St. Augustine Trawlers sails up the San Sebastian River in the summer of 1979. This wooden scallop trawler is also outfitted for shrimping and fishing. Photograph courtesy of St. Augustine Trawlers.

Ships pass before a priest in 1949 during the annual Blessing of the Fleet. The tradition was introduced to St. Augustine in the mid-1940s by shrimpers who learned about the old French custom while trawling in Louisiana. The colorful religious ceremony was revived by Edward Mussallem around 1960, and now attracts almost two hundred vessels to receive the benediction. Photograph courtesy of St. Joseph's Academy.

NO PARKING
Cafe

Opposite Page:
A procession in honor of the consecration of Bishop Thomas Joseph McDonough in 1947 moves down Cathedral Place. Photograph by W. W. Wilson; courtesy of St. Joseph's Academy.

Carpenters, masons, and builders renovate Castle Warden in 1940. Norton Baskin and his wife, Marjorie Kinnan Rawlings, maintained the castle as a hotel and restaurant until 1946. Marjorie Rawlings, known for her authorship of The Yearling, *divided her time between St. Augustine and her house in Cross Creek, about which she also wrote. Photograph courtesy of Geraldine Rowe Maguire.*

The Hotel Castle Warden, pictured in 1946, was built as a residence by William G. Warden for his large family. Warden, a partner of John D. Rockefeller and Henry Flagler, was encouraged by Flagler to invest in the development of St. Augustine. Warden declined, choosing instead to vacation in the city. He constructed the twenty-three-room house which was completed in 1879. It remained in the family through the 1930s, last occupied by Warden's daughter, Elizabeth B. Ketterlinus, for whom a school is named. In 1940 Norton Baskin bought the structure, converting it into a hotel. He sold it in 1946, and, after changing hands several times, the unique edifice was purchased by the present owners, who represent Robert Ripley's "Believe It or Not." Photograph by J. Carver Harris; from the St. Augustine Historical Society.

The city commission of 1946, left to right: Leslie Stevens, city attorney; Herbert E. Wolfe, commissioner; Frank Tart, commissioner; Pauline Boyt, city clerk; Elwood Hartley, fire chief; George Young, mayor; William Lindsey, police chief; Frank Harold, commissioner; Charles Leyvraz, commissioner; Herbert Gooch, city manager. This photograph appeared on the cover of a statewide municipal magazine recognizing the group as the outstanding city commission of the year. Photograph courtesy of the St. Augustine Police Department.

The first snow in thirty-four years chilled St. Augustinians in February 1951. The two-inch snowfall far surpassed the previous record of 0.7 inch in 1917. Photograph from the St. Augustine Historical Society.

Walter B. Fraser (1888-1972), businessman and community leader, served as mayor of St. Augustine in 1934 and 1942. He represented St. Johns County in the senate from 1944 through 1948. The Fountain of Youth and Oldest Wooden School House, local attractions owned by Senator Fraser, still draw visitors to the city. Mannequins in the eighteenth-century frame structure illustrate the house's function as a classroom. The lure of the myth of the fountain of youth draws tourists to a sulfur spring. Also located on the site is an Indian burial ground. Interesting presentations in the planetarium and Globe offer information about the founding of Florida. Photograph from the Florida Photographic Archives, Strozier Library, F. S. U.

F. Charles Usina (1903-66) held a seat in the state House of Representatives for twenty-five years, absent only one term between 1943 and 1966. An athletic field at the Florida School for the Deaf and the Blind commemorates his efforts on behalf of the school. Usina owned and operated the St. Augustine Alligator Farm with partner W. I. Drysdale. Photograph courtesy of the St. Augustine Police Department.

The Kilonaut, *the one thousandth shrimp trawler built by Diesel Engine Sales (Desco), was christened on May 18, 1963. Participating in the ceremony were, left to right: Herbert E. Wolfe, Rosemary Smathers, Senator George A. Smathers, and L. C. Ringhaver. Photograph by Howard Hanson.*

Vice-President Lyndon Johnson greets members of St. Joseph's Academy during his visit to St. Augustine in 1963. Photograph courtesy of St. Joseph's Academy.

A hurricane in 1944 flooded Bay Street, washing the entrance of Usina's dock across the road and up to the Elks Lodge front door. The gate was still securely locked when the owners came to remove their property. Photograph courtesy of Mary (Mrs. Francis) Usina.

From the mid-1950s to 1976 the Fairchild Aircraft Division of Fairchild Engine and Aircraft Construction operated from its Route 1 location north of the city. The industry employed up to six hundred St. Johns County residents to assemble the B-26 aircraft. Photograph by Howard Hanson.

The Conch House Lounge on Anastasia Island replicates Capo's Bath House, the bayfront recreation facility built in 1870 for timid swimmers to paddle about in indoor comfort. The popular bathing spot burned in 1914. The modern representation, built by the Ponces and Steve Kennard, is designed to provide an interesting atmosphere for evening socializing. Drawing courtesy of James A. Ponce, Sr.

The first Easter Festival Queen, Jacquelyn Lopez Young (now McCraw) models the royal dress made in 1960. The gown was worn for several years by each succeeding queen with various alterations and additions. Photograph courtesy of Eleanor Philips Barnes.

Easter Festival

In 1958 horses decorated in flowered bonnets, carriages draped with garlands, and townfolk dressed in spring finery paraded down St. George Street in the first annual Easter Festival. In 1959 an element of distinction was added to the pageantry. A Royal Family was meticulously selected from heritage natives to represent the reigning family in Spain during the years of construction of the Castillo de San Marcos. The objective was two-fold. Attention was drawn to the historic national monument by emphasizing the family responsible for authorizing the fortress. Secondly, the individuals chosen to represent the

King John L. Colee rides before the Castillo in the 1966 Easter Festival. His attendants are Samuel Hodnett, left, and William Baker. Photograph courtesy of Charles Colee.

ruling family were required to prove ancestry dating back to St. Augustine's first Spanish, British, or second Spanish periods. The Family consists of three members: Queen Mariana, who ruled as regent for her young son, Don Carlos, and the boy-king's teenage sister, Margarita. The tradition was originated and supervised in 1959 by director-general Eleanor Philips Barnes. In 1969 responsibility for the unique custom was transferred from Eleanor Barnes to Charles D. Colee, himself a native, expert horseman, and long-time participant in the Royal Family pageantry. The Family reigns for a year, representing St. Augustine throughout the state at numerous functions and celebrations.

King Dan Pacetti stands before the Castillo de San Marcos with past queens and ladies of the court. The dates of reign and heritage family names are listed after each queen. From left to right: Anita W. Hodnett (1960-Capo/Hernandez/Pomar); Joan Nauright, Susie Carcaba, Jacquelyn L. McCraw (1959-Sanchez/Solana/Lopez); Jessica Sparks (1965-Lopez); Princess Maria Mier, Gaby Lee Usina, Mary Menth, Phyllis Trask Thomas (1963-Rogero/Hernandez/Usina); Connie R. Bradshaw. The photograph was taken during the 1965 anniversary year. The inset shows Eleanor Philips Barnes, director-general of the Royal Family for ten years. Photograph courtesy of Eleanor Philips Barnes; inset photograph from the St. Augustine Historical Society.

George William Jackson (1890-1970) made St. Augustine his home at age six when his parents came to Florida from New Jersey. He became deeply involved in the city, its history, and its people, working within its scope his entire life. Jackson was appointed county judge in 1915, the year following acquisition of his law degree from the University of Florida. He served as circuit judge of the Seventh Judicial Circuit from 1927 to 1961. Throughout his fifty years on the bench he maintained a reputation of compassion and consideration for his fellowman. Photograph courtesy of St. Johns County Court House.

The Lion of the Senate, Verle A. Pope, served in the state legislature for twenty-four years, presiding over the Senate during the 1966-68 term. Born in St. Augustine in 1903, Pope fought diligently for his community and was honored for his achievements before his death in 1973. Here he sits between Cornelius Vanderbilt Whitney, right, and Mary Lou Whitney, a couple well known throughout the country but appreciated in Florida for the establishment and development of Marineland, the world's first oceanarium. Norton Baskin, left, is remembered not only as the husband of Marjorie Kinnan Rawlings, but also as the proprietor of the Castle Warden Hotel. Photograph courtesy of Margaret Pope (Mrs. Richard O.) Watson.

Visitors pass through the City Gate, preparing to cross Orange Street as they approach the northern end of restored St. George Street. Photograph courtesy of the St. Augustine Record.

An impressive visitor to St. Augustine was King Juan Carlos de Bourbon, king-designate of Spain, and his wife, Princess Sofia. The couple, center, left, were on a state visit in January 1971, when Charles Colee, left, in costume, presented a folder of photos of St. Augustine's royal trio and a history of the Easter Festival. The woman on the right is an attendant to the princess. Photograph courtesy of Charles Colee.

On colonial St. George Street visitors return to eighteenth-century St. Augustine. On the left stand three restored structures: the Paredes House contains the Old Curiosity Shop; the Rodrigues-Avero-Sanchez House (with flags flying) houses the Museum of Yesterday's Toys; and the Arrivas House includes a silversmith demonstration. Across the street is the De Mesa-Sanchez House, also an extant eighteenth-century structure. The wooden Peso de Burgo-Pellicer House, foreground, is a recent reconstruction offering an eighteenth-century woodworking demonstration. Other exhibits on St. George and adjoining streets include a blacksmith and print shop and demonstrations of weaving, candledipping, and cooking. Occasional demonstrations of crafts such as net-making, palmetto weaving, and lacemaking also delight the public. Photograph courtesy of the St. Augustine Record.

Flowers and trees contributed by the Anderson and Gibbs families adorn the circle which surrounds the Ponce de León statue. Behind Florida's discoverer is the Potter's Wax Museum of historic figures. The reconstructed building at right is St. Augustine Enterprises, a gift shop and information center. Photograph courtesy of the St. Augustine Record.

The reconstructed hospital building on Aviles Street stands on a site once used as Indian burial grounds. Several early Spanish homes were built on the property before 1766, when stables on the lot were converted to a residence by Scotsman William Watson. Watson sold the property to the Spanish government in 1791, when it was used as a pharmacy and infirmary. It became the primary hospital in the city when the main building across the street burned in 1818. Until modern times Aviles Street retained the name of Hospital Street although the stable-hospital was demolished by 1880. A Chinese laundry, a law office, and the Trade Winds cocktail lounge are among the numerous enterprises that have operated from the site. In 1967 the Historic St. Augustine Preservation Board reconstructed the Spanish Military Hospital as a museum. In 1978 the Sandquist art gallery opened with an ever-changing exhibition representing more than fifty artists. Photograph courtesy of the St. Augustine Record.

Like menacing arrowheads, the stone bastions project from the four corners of the solid fortress. It is the still waters of the bay, though, that more accurately reflect the quiet dignity of the historic garrison which maintains an imaginary defense of the ancient city. Photograph courtesy of St. Augustine Record.

A modern view of St. George Street looking south from Hypolita Street reveals a corner of the Casa del Hildago, left foreground, a Spanish-owned information center. Built in 1965 by the Spanish government, the center replicates a typical southern Spain residence that might have been occupied by a sixteenth-century nobleman. The neighboring white house is the Francisco Xavier Sanchez House, owned by the Independent Life Insurance Company. At the far end of the street stands the gray and white Peck House with the Cathedral-Basilica campanile towering above. Photograph by Randy Hoff.

Opposite page:

The Cathedral steeple ascends before Government House in this night photo taken from the top of the Exchange Bank Building in 1951. Photograph by Joseph Dillinger.

Bibliography

Arana, Luis R., and Albert Manucy. *The Building of Castillo de San Marcos.* Philadelphia: Eastern National Park and Monument Association, 1977.

Arnade, Charles W. *The Siege of St. Augustine in 1702.* Gainesville: University of Florida Press, 1959.

Deagen, Kathleen A. "The Archeology of First Spanish Period St. Augustine 1972-1978." *El Escribano,* (1973), pp. 1-22.

Edwards, Virginia. *Stories of Old St. Augustine.* St. Augustine: C. F. Hamblen, Inc., 1973.

Fairbanks, George R. *History and Antiquities of the City of St. Augustine, Florida.* 1858; rpt. Gainsville: University of Florida Press, 1975. [Facsimile edition, introd. Michael V. Gannon.]

Gannon, Michael V. *The Cross in the Sand.* Gainsville: University of Florida Press, 1965.

Gjessing, Frederik. "Observations on the Oldest House." In Gjessing, et. al., *Evolution of the Oldest House, St. Augustine.* Tallahassee: Florida State University, 1962, pp. 107-115.

Graham, Thomas. *The Awakening of St. Augustine.* Tallahassee, Fla.: St. Augustine Historical Society, 1978.

________. "Flagler's Magnificent Hotel Ponce de Leon." *Florida Historical Quarterly,* LIV (July 1975), 1-17.

Manucy, Albert. *Florida's Menendez.* St Augustine: St. Augustine Historical Society, 1965.

________. *The Houses of St. Augustine.* 1962; rpt. Tallahassee: Rose Printing Company, 1978.

Martin, Sidney Walter. *Florida's Flagler.* Athens, Ga.: University of Georgia Press, 1949.

Monteau, A. T. *Coxetterville and Bakersville.* St. Augustine, Fla.: N. p., 1880.

Nason, Elias. *Chapin's Handbook of St. Augustine.* St. Augustine: George H. Chapin, 1884.

Neill, Wilfred T. *Florida's Seminole Indians.* 1952; rpt. St. Petersburg, Fla: N. p., 1976.

Panagopoulos, E. P. *New Smyrna: An Eighteenth Century Greek Odyssey.* Brookline, Massachusetts: Holy Cross Orthodox Press, 1966.

Quinn, Jane. *Minorcas in Florida.* St. Augustine, Fla.: Mission Press, 1975.

Redding, David A. *Flagler and His Church.* Jacksonville, Fla.: Paramount Press, 1970.

Speissegger, R. A. *Early History of New Augustine.* St. Augustine, Fla.: Private printing, 1953.

Tebeau, Charlton W. *A History of Florida.* Coral Gables, Fla.: University of Miami Press, 1976.

Van Campen, J. T. *St. Augustine: Florida's Colonial Capital.* St. Augustine, Fla.: St. Augustine Historical Society, 1959.

Watt, Margaret Gibbs. *The Gibbs Family of Long Ago and Near at Hand 1337-1967.* Jacksonville, Fla.: Paramount Press, 1967.

Wright, J. Leitch, Jr. *British St. Augustine.* St. Augustine, Fla.: Historic St. Augustine Preservation Board, 1975.

Index